The Enemy

The Double-Edge Sword of our Inner-Self

Henry Zephirin

Printed in the United States of America.
ISBN: 9798287095376

ACKNOWLEDGMENTS

I dedicate this book to my deceased father and mother, watching from above, saying: "If only he practices half of what he is writing, then we have not done too badly. He is not a lost cause, after all." To them, I attribute much of my ethics and morals that allow me to acknowledge my errors, right my wrongs, and make lemonades out of lemons.

I thank my sister, Micheline, whose support and patience reflect her unswerving dedication and commitment towards me and the family. Her work ethic is unsurpassed, her determination is legendary, and her resilience is inspiring. She brings out the best example of what "Loyalty" means.

To my children, Louis, Vanessa, Alexandra, and Michelle, this book affirms that learning is continuous, sharing knowledge and helping others are worthy endeavors, and perfection of character resulting in noble citizenship is a lifetime goal.

Over the years, several individuals recommended I write a book. None of these individuals would imagine the book's name or topics. However, after observing human traits that betrayed people's intent and revealed the fundamental nature of a person, it was clear the book's content would be informative.

I send heartfelt thanks to Susan Collins—my confidante, significant other, and constant companion through all the highs and lows. Her continuous encouragement, unrelenting work ethic, and upbeat attitude have given me courage and made me laugh throughout. I will always be thankful to her for embodying the light, devotion, and humor that this journey demanded.

Lastly, I will always appreciate the invisible and unnamed people who have influenced me along the way, particularly over the past decades, and still do and always will.

CONTENTS

INTRODUCTION

I bet when you saw the title of the book, The Enemy.... you thought you were going to read about war. In a way, you'd be right. But this book isn't about the battlefields of WWI or WWII, nor is it about the more recent war in Afghanistan that has cost 1,900 US soldiers their lives. It is not set in the Highlands of Vietnam, nor in the deserts of Iraq.

The conflict we will discuss does not involve bullets or bombs. Instead, it's fought with ideology, culture, and politics. It's turned entire nations into battlegrounds. Worsened by social media, which constantly creates outrage and fuels endless skirmishes between opposing sides, this battle has seen families and friendships fracture under the weight of irreconcilable beliefs. Now, in an age where words wound as profoundly as weapons and enemies seem to multiply daily, this fight is only getting more complex.

The fight I'm talking about isn't one you'll have been taught about in school. It's not there in the history books. It is far more personal, insidious, and deceptive. It has shaped civilizations, destroyed dreams, and held people captive for centuries.

It is the war within.

We are all quick to blame external forces for our failures - bad luck, an unfair boss, a toxic relationship, an economy that never seems to work in our favor. We tell ourselves that circumstances aren't quite right. We dream about a fair world and think if only the right opportunities would come our way. Maybe then, we would be happy, successful, and fulfilled. We convince ourselves that the enemy is always outside us - that it's got to be someone else, something else, an obstacle beyond our control.

But what if that isn't true?

Have you ever considered that the enemy may not be out there but within you?

Hiding behind our own defenses, the real enemy does not carry an insignia or possess a rifle. It lurks stealthily in your thoughts, molding them, complicating your beliefs and perceptions, and completely eradicating your self-esteem. It is the force that instructs us to surrender before we've even started trying, and that amplifies all of our self-doubts until they ultimately outweigh our self-belief.

It's the reason we hesitate, the reason we settle, the reason we let life slip through our fingers while we wait for that moment of certainty that never comes.

This book is about unmasking that enemy.

It's about understanding how our minds can be our greatest adversaries and yet, paradoxically, our most powerful allies.

This book will help you understand our harmful habits, the boundaries we set for ourselves, and the deeply embedded fears that govern our actions. More crucially, it will provide the guidance needed to end this cycle of self-sabotage and, instead of fighting the world, show you how to turn that fight inward and battle the inner demons that restrict you from becoming the best version of yourself.

I have included an Appendix where I present the educational and socio-political implications of the traits discussed. I follow this with a Theoretical Framework summarizing my precept with the acronym TRAPPED. I leave you with a visual connection that frees you from the confines of the TRAPPED model and towards the path to conquering the enemy within.

By the end of this book, you'll understand that the enemy within is a double-edged sword; it can destroy or sharpen us. The choice is ours.

So, it's time to stop searching for the answers before asking the right question. It's time to stop wondering who your enemy is and ask: Are you ready to face the enemy within?

The Seven Traits That Define Our Inner Enemy

If the enemy within is the greatest threat to our potential, we must ask: what form does this enemy take?

There is no specific vision of the enemy within. Instead, it hides behind traits we often admire—the very qualities we associate with strength, determination, and success.

This allows the enemy to hide from us. It doesn't attack with brute force. It operates subtly, weaving into our thoughts, choices, and identities. When unchecked, the enemy convinces us that we are correct when we are, in fact, dangerously wrong, that we are in control when we are actually spiraling out of control, and that we're moving forward when we're standing still and stagnating.

The enemy within is defined by seven core traits: ego, passion, rationalization, perfection, pride, tradition, and loyalty. Each of these traits, when harnessed wisely, can serve us as powerful tools.

When we fail to harness them, though, they can run rampant. At this point, we give these traits a chance to sway our judgment, ruin our perceptions, and sabotage our chances of success.

To examine how this happens and how we can tackle it, we first must analyze each of these seven traits. We need to understand how each of them manifests, how they work against us, and how we can strive to reclaim control over them.

In pursuit of such analysis, each chapter of this book will include:

- Invaluable analysis of the characteristics and influence of each trait.

- Real-world case studies illustrate each trait's dangers.

- Actionable steps you can take to take each trait from an enemy to an ally.

The time has come to beat the enemy within. By confronting these seven traits head-on, we can completely reshape our inner world and, in turn, our external reality.

Let's examine the first—and most deceptive—trait: **ego.**

CHAPTER 1
EGO IS THE ENEMY OF COMMON SENSE

"Ego is the anesthesia that deadens the pain of stupidity."
— Rick Rigsby

In every era, ego has proven to be a formidable adversary. It whispers false assurances of invincibility, blinding individuals and institutions to their reality, and leading to easily preventable disasters. An unchecked ego can turn strength into weakness. To prevent this, we need to master our ego; the first step is to understand it.

Understanding Ego and Its Hidden Danger

At the simplest level, our ego works as our perception of identity, self-importance, and superiority. It is responsible for how we view ourselves, especially in relation to others and the world around us. By doing so, ego influences everything. It can impact our decisions and even alter our opinions and beliefs. Its job is to act as our internal storyteller, sitting behind the scenes in our consciousness and creating narratives about who we are, what we're worth, and comparing us to everyone else in our lives.

This might seem necessary or perhaps even worthwhile. For many people, ego is essential. When you have a hold on it, the ego is a valuable tool that helps fuel ambition, boost confidence, and motivate people to succeed. A healthy sense of self-worth and a little competition with others can be really beneficial, after all.

However, there is more to our ego than there may seem. Beneath what seems like a helpful tool is a hidden danger. Ego, when left unchecked, can be responsible for distorting our perception of reality, quietly turning what was once confidence into complacency, conviction into stubbornness, and self-belief into a dangerous illusion of invulnerability. All of which it does without us noticing; ego's biggest danger lies in its subtlety. It does not announce itself loudly like anger or manifest as overt arrogance. Instead, unchecked ego operates quietly from within, slowly working away until it has completely undermined our ability to perceive our reality objectively.

Ego can affect our common sense—at its core, common sense is our ability to assess reality accurately and weigh risks sensibly to recognize our limitations. Ego directly opposes this. When ego runs rampant, we can quickly become almost over-convinced of ourselves. We start believing we are uniquely gifted, inherently wiser, or somehow immune to the pitfalls and mistakes that so easily affect others. Despite what we may assume, this warped view doesn't stem from arrogance or pride but rather from an internal conviction that our abilities, talents, or past successes simply exempt us from rules, risks, and rational caution.

This distorted perception of ourselves pushes us to disregard any and all opposing viewpoints, ignore advice, and even dismiss valuable insights from others. An ego-driven mind cannot function in the way any normal consciousness would. When ego runs rampant, we perceive feedback as criticism, opposing viewpoints as threats, and cautionary advice as unnecessary interference. Our ego begins to convince us that we already have all the answers, which encourages us to overlook critical warnings, dismiss valuable insights, and discard those whose perspectives challenge our newly inflated self-perception.

However, the biggest issue with ego is that it rarely appears problematic until the damage is already done. Its slow and steady impact on our common sense quietly prevents us from recognizing any warning signs or acknowledging any of our errors until the subsequent consequences become unavoidable and severe. It isn't unheard of for organizations, leaders, and even ordinary individuals to overlook the ego's subtle influence until faced with undeniable failures it has left in its wake, such as financial ruin, relationship breakdowns, or catastrophic mistakes.

Let us consider for a moment a business executive who dismisses a colleague's cautionary advice, convinced that their past successes guarantee positive future outcomes. They may feel that their internal conviction and sense of sureness is justified; in fact, they may even feel like it is inspirational or motivational in some way. However, their attitude eventually becomes a barrier to adaptability and innovation. They stop being open to feedback, and slowly but surely, their ability to adjust strategically, think on the spot, and course correct all begin to wither—all because their ego has convinced them they don't need those skills. Similarly, ego quietly encourages us to dismiss valid criticisms and even perceive other people's feelings as attacks in personal relationships. This can lead to a refusal to apologize, which contributes to bubbling tensions and barriers between us and them, all of which could have been avoided through humility and self-awareness.

Ego's all-important distinction from related traits like pride or arrogance only further demonstrates its nature as a hidden threat. Pride is externally focused, largely looking for external validation and acknowledgment. Arrogance is the open expression of this superiority and is a visible sign that is easy to recognize and challenge. Ego, alternatively, works within, convincing us privately of our superiority. It is subtle, internalized, and so it becomes much more complex to detect, like the aforementioned.

Therefore, to effectively confront ego, self-awareness becomes critical. We must learn how to recognize when our ego is steering our decisions, attitudes and interactions. We must spot when we're being steered away from reason. This process begins with consciously questioning our motivations, honestly examining our emotional reactions, and actively seeking external perspectives—particularly when we feel most certain and self-assured.

In summary, ego's most significant danger lies in its invisibility and subtlety. It quietly corrodes judgment, distorts perception, and convinces us that caution, feedback, and humility are unnecessary. Recognizing and mastering ego requires constant vigilance, honest self-reflection, and genuine humility. By understanding its hidden danger, we gain the power to harness ego's beneficial qualities—confidence, ambition, and self-belief—while protecting ourselves from its silent and destructive influence.

The Cost of Ego-Driven Decision

Case Study #1 - The Titanic: A Tragedy of Overconfidence

This is a story we're all familiar with. Or, at least, you think you're familiar with it. It is a tragic story that took place in April 1912 when passengers boarded the RMS Titanic. Once on board, they marveled at the ship's opulence, and professionals drooled over its engineering prowess. Dubbed "unsinkable," it was a true feat of engineering wonder, or so it seemed. To many, it represented humanity's triumph, the entrance of society into a golden age of travel, creation, and industry. On its maiden voyage from Southampton to New York, the Titanic was more than just a ship. It was a symbol. Wealthy passengers relaxed on her decks, danced in grand ballrooms, and dined more lavishly than most people back on land.

But we all know that's not where the story ended. There was more going on behind the scenes. Dangerous complacency, rooted in ego, had determined the Titanic's fate before she'd even launched.

Her captain determined a large part of the Titanic's fate. Captain Edward Smith, known as the "Millionaire's Captain" for his popularity among the ultra-wealthy, had been given the job. With a long, reputable career, it made sense. He was a well-known name among the travelers on the ship, and he was due to retire, so the launch of the Titanic seemed a suitable last voyage for a man of his tenure. However, on the journey, Smith decided to maintain top cruising speeds even after receiving numerous iceberg warnings from nearby ships. He was confident that the ship's sheer size and the visibility from the helm would keep them safe. Changing the route or acting accordingly would've slowed them down. It would've forever changed the reputation of the Titanic and his role as captain. Instead, he opted for a timely arrival to protect his ego, forgoing the usual concern and care required at sea.

It wasn't just Smith, though. The shipbuilders also allowed their egos to overrule necessary safety measures. The Titanic was only ever equipped with twenty lifeboats, fewer than half the correct amount for the 2,224 onboard passengers. The builders thought lifeboats were an unnecessary blemish on the ship's magnificent appearance, so they simply decided not to add them. In fact, the builders actually thought that adding more lifeboats would inspire fear and suggest insecurity. So they left a boat with over 2,000 passengers with twenty lifeboats to save them.

Unbeknownst to passengers, other shortcuts were taken during construction, too. Substandard iron rivets were chosen for speed and convenience, which compromised the integrity of the Titanic's hull. Workers voiced concerns when installing them but were dismissed by supervisors who cared more about deadlines and achieving the launch of the largest and fastest ship ever crafted.

The culmination of this ego-led madness came to fruition on April 14. As the Titanic sped through the North Atlantic, the crew spotted an iceberg just a moment too late. They frantically rushed to do all they could do to move the ship and save the passengers, but it soon became clear that the collision was unavoidable. To start with, the Titanic's reputation reassured everyone, subduing the panic. It couldn't be anything serious, not with such a strong, tall, fast ship and an expert captain—right?

Then chaos erupted. The untrained crew struggled to launch the few lifeboats effectively. Even when they could launch the lifeboats, many passengers were confused and misinformed, and many chose to stay aboard the Titanic, assuming that the Titanic was a safer option.

Within less than three hours, the Titanic sank, claiming over 1,500 lives in what was easily one of maritime history's most tragic—and avoidable—disasters. The loss of life was entirely preventable, and while it may seem to many it was the result of the iceberg, it is clearly deeper than that. The sinking of the Titanic resulted from ego, arrogance and the tragic abandonment of common sense. The disaster that occurred starkly illustrates ego's fatal flaw: it can completely blind us to risks, leading to the dismissal of critical warnings and ultimately ensuring failure.

The Titanic's sinking ignited widespread outrage and profound grief, fundamentally changing maritime safety regulations. Its legacy is a somber reminder: unchecked ego is far more dangerous than any external threat. The Titanic's tragic story endures not simply as a maritime disaster but as a powerful lesson in humility and the relentless necessity of common sense.

Case Study #2: Charlemagne - The Emperor Who Overestimated His Own Strength

Charlemagne stands as a towering figure in European history, a colossus whose influence is to thank for the course of much of the continent. Crowned Emperor of Romans in 800 AD by Pope Leo III, Charlemagne was responsible for the unification of much of Western Europe after the fall of the Roman Empire. His influence spanned modern-day France, Germany, Italy and beyond, an empire that signaled a new era. Under his guidance, Europe witnessed a flourishing revival in everything from art to education. The era later became known as the Carolingian Renaissance.

But it wasn't all growth and flourish. Charlemagne undoubtedly had a wealth of indisputable accomplishments but eventually fell victim to the hidden danger within us all—ego.

As the emperor aged, his authority went unquestioned, and his power only continued to prove limitless. By the time he was elderly, he had become certain that he was invulnerable, infallible. Advisors who had previously held influence over his decisions, who had given him valuable insight that he'd used to gain and remain in power, were now being ignored. Prudent warnings from those close to him were lost on him, as he believed that his wisdom alone had propelled his empire and him to greatness.

This was to be the downfall of his legacy. During the last years of Charlemagne's reign, his closest counselor, Alcuin of York, warned him of the empire's vulnerability. He urged the emperor to create a solid, robust succession plan. Alcuin told Charlemagne that an empire's true strength lay not in the power of one man but in the stability and continuity of its governance. Charlemagne wouldn't hear it. He was sure that he knew better and that his accomplishments were enough to secure his legacy forever.

So, when it came to his succession, he split his empire across his three sons. He split his land between his three sons. He did not give them any instructions regarding unity or collaboration. He did not bother to cast one heir, instead trusting familial bonds and his sons' respect for all he had done when alive. In doing so, he failed to consider ambition and sibling rivalry.

When Charlemagne passed in 811 AD, the consequences of his oversight did not take long to arise. His eldest son, Louis the Pious, immediately assumed control, but it was clear he could not manage his brothers' ambitions. Soon, what started as internal conflicts escalated into a full-blown civil war. Fueled by their egos, the sons tore apart their father's legacy, convinced they had the right to rule.

What had once been a united and prosperous empire was splintered into fragments. The aftermath of the ego-fueled rampage ushered in a turbulent era of feudalism marked by violence, instability, and political fragmentation, all of which plagued the continent for centuries. Charlemagne's ego-driven failure to plan his succession plunged an entire continent into nothing short of prolonged conflict, a direct consequence of ego overshadowing practicality and common sense.

Plenty of historical records from this period vividly recount the tragedy. Chroniclers wrote in despair about the endless skirmishes and sudden loss of stability across Europe, lamenting how swiftly the mighty had fallen. Charlemagne's empire became more of a warning of the dangers of one's ego than a lasting testament to his achievements.

The lasting legacy of Charlemagne's mistake is reflected in the conflict that followed it and in the lesson it can teach leaders today. Power and success, no matter how immense, are fragile when they are not grounded in practicality, long-term strategic thinking, and humility. Ego had twisted Charlemagne's perception, and had convinced him that his legacy was untouchable. It blinded him to the reality that genuine greatness demands careful planning beyond one's lifetime.

The fall of Charlemagne's empire was not caused by external threats or internal incompetence but by the insidious and silent threat of ego. It is another timeless reminder that unchecked ego can and will destroy the accomplishments it seeks to glorify.

Case Study #3 - Blockbuster vs. Netflix: Hubris in the Digital Age

Blockbuster Video stood as an undisputed titan in home entertainment in the late 1990s and early 2000s. It was a cultural phenomenon, boasting over 9,000 stores worldwide. At its peak, walking into a Blockbuster store was an experience: bright luminescent lights, aisles filled to the brim with the latest Hollywood hits, and enthusiastic clerks helping customers find the best weekend entertainment to suit them. Blockbuster felt like more than just a video rental store. It embodied the weekend family ritual, date night preparation, and spontaneous movie nights.

Its time in the limelight, however, was limited. It was limited by a dangerous complacency fueled by ego. In 2000, Reed Hastings and Marc Randolph, the co-founders of Netflix, a then-unknown media company, approached Blockbuster CEO John Antioco. They offered to sell Netflix for $50 million. Famously, Antioco rejected the offer and laughed the Netflix team out of his office. He had confidence in his retail giant, so much confidence that he could not believe that a fledgling DVD-by-mail subscription model could ever replace the tangible, immediate gratification provided by his brick-and-mortar stores.

Many of Antioco's colleagues within Blockbuster's leadership shared his arrogance. They considered their position at the top unassailable, dismissing the new and innovative Netflix business model as niche and simply unsustainable. As a group, they were convinced that customers valued the in-store experience, ignoring their customers' growing frustration with late fees and a limited selection.

Undeterred by one rejection, Netflix innovated and adapted to customer demands. They started refining their DVD-by-mail service, using detailed analytics to understand customer preferences. By 2007, sensing the shift in the market, Netflix made the bold move to pivot to online streaming—a technological leap that many industry experts looked at with concern and skepticism.

Blockbuster, in stark contrast, made no movement. The company hesitated while executives debated internally, bogged down by a sense of security. Their stubborn refusal to acknowledge what was clearly a shift in market dynamics resulted in a final, last-ditch attempt at a half-hearted online rental service too late and too reluctantly. Their efforts were superficial and desperate, whereas Netflix had been strategic and had used their foresight.

By 2010, the tide had turned. Blockbuster had been synonymous with home entertainment but had now filed for bankruptcy. The company closed down thousands of stores, laying off tens of thousands of employees in the process. The company's downfall was quick and, honestly, nothing short of humiliating. It was a direct consequence of John Antioco's ego-led shortsightedness.

In the meantime, Netflix flourished. Without ego or arrogance holding it back, the company transformed ad bloomed into a global entertainment powerhouse with over 200 million subscribers. Netflix executives consistently attribute their success not to certainty but to humility and the willingness to acknowledge that they may not have all the answers.

All these years later, Blockbuster's story is not just about a failed business but also a cautionary tale of ego's destructive potential. It reminds us how easily our success can breed arrogance and how, in those situations, our ego can blind us to change and innovation. By convincing us we know better, we dull our senses

Blockbuster's fall was avoidable. If its leaders prioritize humility, adaptability,, and innovation, they may still have a business today. Instead, they let their ego insist they were too big to fail, too dominant to be replaced, and too successful to learn from a newcomer like Netflix. Their collapse once again underscores that essential lesson: success demands humility.

The Netflix versus Blockbuster story is just another painful example of how ego transforms strength into weakness and success into downfall. It shows us another leader who struggled to remain vigilant and strong against the subtle whispers of ego.

This case study shows that ego distorts our reality, blinding companies to market shifts. Blockbuster refused to adapt, to accept change. They assumed that their past success would guarantee future dominance.

But they failed to remember that adaptation is key. If you don't adapt, you don't survive.

You can have confidence in your beliefs and still listen; listening will always matter. Blockbuster dismissed Netflix without hearing, without considering the potential that Netflix had—and it cost them everything.

Mastering Ego: Action Steps for Staying Grounded

Those case studies may all be from the past but don't be fooled into thinking that the ego is a purely historical enemy. Ego works on a daily basis, influencing how we feel, what we believe, and even what we do. Whether you're running a business, managing your personal growth, or making a life-changing decision—doing so with an unchecked ego is risky.

To avoid taking these risks, you must master the double-edged sword that ego presents. Practice humility and follow some of these actionable tasks.

1. Seek Feedback

Proactively seeking feedback from those in our lives is one of the best ways to keep your ego in check. It's a simple yet extraordinarily effective tool, especially when we seek out the opinions of those who aren't guaranteed to offer praise, who may challenge our point of view and put our ego (and us) in our place.

Doing this is vital in ensuring we are not lost in an echo chamber. Demanding feedback from a wide range of people helps ensure that we are not inadvertently reinforcing blindspots that we may not even know we have. This prevents us from creating an image of ourselves and our perspective as completely invulnerable and infallible, reinforcing the story that our unchecked ego wants us to believe.

Our ego wants us to believe we are right and the only opinion worth listening to. So, when we take on others' opinions, that means absorbing and taking on their perspective, not just hearing it.

You cannot grow if you don't process the information given to you. This may not come quickly—it is a skill many people have to learn. Listening to criticism without defensiveness is a hallmark of emotional maturity. Acting upon these insights and this feedback demonstrates a genuine willingness to grow, improve, and evolve, distinguishing exceptional individuals from those who stagnate.

2. Embrace Uncertainty

Ego thrives in perceived certainty. When we think we know everything and believe we can't be surprised or proven wrong, our ego grows. It starts to foster complacency and rigidity within us—as, after all, why do we need to change what we're doing or listen to anyone else when we know everything?

So, to battle our ego effectively, we have to embrace uncertainty. We must accept that true wisdom lies in recognizing that we don't know everything and that our knowledge is always incomplete. Learning, indeed, is an ongoing journey that has no final destination. As human beings, we don't know everything there is to know, so how could we be sure as individuals?

Accepting this state of mind and seeking out new knowledge is a great way to grow and develop and, in turn, keep ego at bay. Humility will be vital in fighting our egos if we can admit to ourselves and others we don't have all the answers and can adapt as necessary.

3. Acknowledge Your Limits

Acknowledging our limitations is an ego-killer. Turning around and admitting fault and admitting weakness is a surefire way to rein our ego back in.

Confidence in ourselves and our work is great, but like wisdom, true strength comes from understanding that we can't do it all. We must understand and recognize our strengths and weaknesses and know that we are not diminishing our strengths or value by doing so.

Acknowledging where our pitfalls are makes us wiser; it makes us better team players, better at making decisions, and better compensated for those pitfalls. By spotting and familiarizing ourselves with these elements of ourselves, we can choose to be around people who excel in areas we don't, and whose strengths complement ours. This enables us to learn from them and develop those skills rather than avoid them, thus avoiding stagnation altogether.

4. Learn from Mistakes

Our ego hates failure. It forces us to hate failure and see it as irredeemable, a calamity. When, in reality, we should see failure as a growth opportunity. We should strive to learn from our mistakes, not fear them. What separates successful individuals who are not ruled by their ego from those who are is their willingness to evaluate failure and find meaningful lessons.

We develop resilience by reflecting on our past, identifying what went wrong, and how we can improve. We learn by taking personal responsibility for these failures, not looking to blame external factors. Only when ego takes hold do we blame the latter, and this causes us to freeze. We can't learn from mistakes we do not believe are ours.

We must view setbacks as stepping stones rather than permanent calamitous defeats to free ourselves from the grips of ego's hidden dangers. This will encourage us to grow, giving us the strength to face future challenges and failures rather than hiding from our mistakes and shirking the responsibility, ultimately burying our heads in the sand and letting life pass us by.

5. Stay Focused on the Bigger Picture

Ego is all about immediate personal validation—short-term wins where it is fed recognition, praise, and status. The ego fixates on these short-term accolades; if we let them, it blinds us to the true goal and the bigger picture.

However, focusing on the bigger picture is essential for success. Prioritizing immediate wins over long-term sustainability or impact is destined to fail, and that's where ego leaves us.

Lasting success demands we look at the bigger picture and keep our eye on the prize. The most established leaders emphasize and thrive off of collaboration over competition. They set aside pride and validation for long-term, consistent, and collective success.

To keep ego at bay, we must hold onto the image of the big picture, the idea that we are reaching for, the goal that got us started.

Choosing Humility over Hubris

Opting for humility over hubris is about embracing that we won't have all the answers and accepting feedback with openness rather than a defense. It's about acknowledging our limits without shame and viewing our failures as a learning experience, not an obstacle.

It's all about remembering that humility isn't weakness—it's wisdom! Those who master the double-sided sword that is ego can remain grounded and open-minded, ultimately helping them to achieve greatness. When our ego rules us, we can't reach such heights as we believe success is guaranteed, and we will always struggle to attain it.

Key Takeaways

- Ego distorts reality and blinds us to essential warnings.
- Overconfidence can turn strength into weakness.
- Humility is the key to sustained success.
- True leaders acknowledge their limitations and learn from feedback.

Final Thoughts: The Silent Saboteur of Success

Ego is far more vicious than a personal weakness or a character flaw. It's a hidden enemy capable of taking hold of a person's life and completely ruining them. It operates silently, just out of sight, influencing us more than we could ever expect. It can impact everything from mundane parts of our life, changing small things like daily choices to moments that define us and our careers.

History is full to the brim with examples of people and businesses that fell victim to ego's tricks and seduction.

The Titanic did not sink because of just an iceberg; it sank because of an unshakable belief in its invincibility. This was an unfounded belief that came to override common sense and safety protocols, leading to a historical tragedy and a timeless lesson. The Titanic teaches that no matter how successful we become, ego is the iceberg beneath the surface, waiting for us to let our guard down for just long enough to cause havoc.

Charlemagne did not lose his Empire because of a single weak successor but because he failed to acknowledge that even the strongest rulers needed to plan for their death.

Blockbuster did not fall because Netflix was an ultimately superior company or because superior men ran it. It fell because it was too arrogant, too wrapped up in ego, to see change coming.

Ego takes us out of reality and stops us from understanding. Those who adapt, question themselves and recognize their limitations are the ones who reap the rewards. It is not hiding behind arrogance and believing failure to be impossible that leads us into the arms of success, but planning, learning, and developing.

From the arrogant dismissal of carefully planned safety measures aboard the Titanic to the shortsighted assumption that family alone would connect an empire, the common thread is clear: ego distorts judgment, undermines intelligence, and blinds even the most sensible and well-prepared people to risks and warnings.

Ego is the hidden danger that convinces us that we are superior; therefore, the rules of failure do not apply to us. It tells us lies, convincing us that we are too good to make fatal mistakes, too experienced to be caught off guard. But history clearly tells another story.

Ego makes us feel invulnerable. It is reassuring and comforting. When we're at our most vulnerable, it completely blinds us to it. It often masquerades as self-confidence, but the line between the two is impossibly thin.

No individual, organization, or empire is immune. Even the strongest, wisest, and most successful among us face the risk of ego-driven disaster. To assume otherwise is to fall into the trap that countless others have fallen into before us.

The challenge we all face is not the absence of ego but managing it. There is no removing ego from our minds, our bodies or our consciousness. Keeping ego in check is a lifelong effort, requiring vigilance, self-awareness, and humility. It involves surrounding ourselves with honest voices, embracing uncertainty, learning from all of our mistakes, and focusing on the greater good rather than personal glory.

The ego can be a powerful force when controlled. In the right hands, ego drives ambition, fuels determination, and fosters great success. It is only when it is left unchecked that it becomes this hidden, vicious enemy.

Every day presents a choice: we can either master our ego or let it master us. Those who choose the path of humility, openness, and continuous learning are the ones who achieve lasting success and meaningful impact.

Ask yourself clearly and honestly:

Are you controlling your ego, or is your ego controlling you?

Your answer will shape your destiny.

CHAPTER 2: PASSION IS THE ENEMY OF REASON

Understanding Passion and Its Hidden Danger

Passion is often associated with great achievements. From heroic acts to groundbreaking innovation, plenty of people who have received thanks and status from their peers have done so because of their passion. It is often assumed to be an essential ingredient for outstanding achievements—and it isn't hard to see why.

However, passion's darker side isn't spoken about as freely. Often hidden beneath the alluring promise of success, drive, and excitement, this side of passion can escalate into intense emotional states. These moments of intense emotion can blind people to rational thought, and even undermine their ability to complete objective analysis of what's going on around them, which can lead to destructive outcomes.

Passion becomes dangerous when it crosses from focused motivation into something more. When not watched, passion can breed impatience, recklessness, and stubbornness. It can become an unchecked obsession, an unruly and brute force that can lead people awry. When left to go 'wild,' it can distort judgment, making people impulsive, even at the expense of logic and reasoning. This facet of passion, this darker side, is the second trait we will be examining as part of the enemy within.

Standard healthy enthusiasm and passion differ in their relationship to reason and self-control. A healthy enthusiasm for something includes balance, decision-making backed by transparency and logic, and a measured approach to achieving goals. It is associated with a steady motivation, resilience to setbacks as and when they arise, and an openness to feedback. A healthy enthusiasm should energize a person without overwhelming their ability to remain objective. With enthusiasm on our side, we should be able to pursue our ambitions sustainably rather than impulsively.

On the other hand, people purely fueled by passion often ignore rational considerations and inflate emotional responses. It makes us volatile and activates powerful emotions and desires that seem to overshadow everything else. Caution, critical thinking, and compromise get thrown to the wind, and our mindset becomes rigid. So much so that obstacles become threats rather than growth opportunities, we lose any sense of adaptability. This fuel type often runs out quickly, and without passion, we are just burnt out, frustrated, and frequently even self-destructive.

We must recognize the difference between these two states. Enthusiasm and passion may seem like they come hand in hand, but in reality, they are two sides of the same coin—one will give you what you need to achieve your goals, and one may feel like that but will burn you out and make you your own worst enemy before you know it.

We can channel our passion into productive and healthy enthusiasm by cultivating self-awareness. We can embrace the motivation it provides while holding tightly onto our reason and logic. This will help us to harness the positive aspects of passion and to ride the wave to achieve our goals.

The Cost of Passion-Driven Decisions

History is filled with decisions made in moments of passion that have resulted in devastating personal, organizational, and even national consequences. When our emotions take control, they overshadow our judgment and cause us to make impulsive decisions that ignore risks and impacts.

Leaders who have allowed passion to fuel their decisions have historically confused their conviction with correctness, dismissing evidence and warnings as mere obstacles and opposition. Organizations caught up in the fires of passion have frequently been caught overlooking policies and considerations like ethical standards or safety concerns. It isn't just at a political and organizational level that passion can have an impact, though. Personal relationships also suffer when passion overrides reason, leading to misunderstandings, arguments, and, more often than not, irreversible harm.

Ultimately, passion-driven decisions can lead to all sorts of catastrophes. Passion can completely tear apart reputations; in some situations, even lives and nations can be irreparably damaged. Looking at these examples throughout history, the crucial importance of not trusting passion alone is evident, as is the necessity of holding on tightly to rational thought.

Case Study #4 - Napoleon Bonaparte and the Russian Campaign: When Ambition Outstripped Logic

Napoleon Bonaparte, one of history's most celebrated military commanders, is both famous and infamous for his encounters with passion and its dual nature. Known for being a tactical genius, a charismatic leader, and being full of boundless ambition, Napoleon rose from obscurity and became the Emperor of France. As the emperor, he built an empire that completely reshaped the map of Europe.

The passion and ambition that got him to that point, though, completely blinded him, leading him to his greatest military blunder—the invasion of Russia in 1812.

Early that year, Napoleon stood at the height of his power. Driven by an insatiable passion and a desire for dominance, he set his sights on conquering Russia, hoping it would cement his control over continental Europe. His advisors, all seasoned generals, and strategists, begged him to be cautious. They presented valid concerns about Russia's vast geography, harsh climate, and the many logistical challenges other conquerors had ignored and fell victim to. Napoleon's passion overrode their logical pleas, and he dismissed warnings as cowardice or lack of ambition.

Confident that he could not fail, largely due to the passion fueling him, Napoleon assembled one of the largest forces in history. The Grand Armee comprised nearly 600,000 soldiers drawn from across various conquered territories. The force was equipped with heavy artillery and extensive supplies and was expected to overwhelm Russia quickly, compelling the Tsar into submission. Napoleon expected a quick, decisive victory that would cement his legacy.

However, the Russians had anticipated the attack. They employed a scorched-earth policy, strategically retreating and destroying crops, livestock, and villages, leaving Napoleon's massive force vulnerable as they marched eastward across the Niemen River.

Napoleon didn't stop, though. Passion pushed him further into enemy territory, disregarding the logistical issues, the stretched supplies, and declining morale. Each step he took magnified each issue tenfold until September, when they finally reached Moscow. Expecting a decisive battle or a negotiated surrender, Napoleon found the ancient city completely abandoned. It had been set on fire by retreating Russians, meaning it offered no shelter and even less of a strategic advantage.

Napoleon's stubborn pride prolonged the invasion. He delayed retreat, utterly convinced that Tsar Alexander I would eventually surrender. Days became weeks as his passion turned to pride. He ignored very clear signs of impending disaster, and as his supplies dwindled, his once confident army became demoralized, restless, and nervous as the Russian winter approached.

Napoleon was forced into a belated retreat in October as the Grand Armee confronted Russia's brutal winter season. Merciless cold, starvation, disease, and relentless guerrilla attacks from the Russians sent Napoleon's soldiers into despair. Every day in Russian territory was a battle for survival. Thousands of soldiers succumbed daily, and others deserted and surrendered. Still, Napoleon rode stoically through his diminished ranks, refusing to accept any responsibility for the catastrophe his unruly, unchecked passion had caused.

By the time the army—or what was left of it—left Russia, fewer than 50,000 of the original 600,000 soldiers had survived. The Russian Campaign devastated Napoleon's army and shattered his reputation of invincibility. It marked the beginning of the end for

Napoleon's empire.

The Russian campaign's tragedy demonstrates passion's peril when divorced from rationality. Napoleon's intelligence and experience didn't save him or his soldiers from the results of his passion-led campaign. His judgment and inability to weigh risks objectively were utterly clouded. No number of opposing views could turn his head or convince him it was time for a strategic pivot when the situation rapidly worsened. His relentless passion turned ambition caused him to overlook risk, leading to catastrophic vulnerabilities. His attempt on Russia is a grim reminder of how unchecked emotional fervor can distort even the sharpest minds.

Today, historians describe the Russian disaster as an archetypal example of passion and greed overpowering reason. It is used frequently as a cautionary tale for leaders and decision-makers across all fields. It reminds us that passion must always be paired with humility, careful planning, and an open mind. Otherwise, passion runs too freely and quickly goes from being a prime source of fuel for our ambition to the cause of our downfall.

Napoleon Bonaparte's Russian Campaign endures through history not merely as a catastrophe but as an enduring lesson. It teaches us that true greatness requires a delicate balance of passion and reason.

Case Study #5 - Enron Corporation: When Passion for Profit Overshadowed Reason

In the late 20th century, the Enron Corporation was more than just another energy company—it was a global phenomenon. Founded by Kenneth Lay in 1985, Enron swiftly climbed the ranks, soon becoming known for its innovation, rapid growth, and economic prowess.

With charismatic leaders Kenneth Lay and later CEO Jeffrey Skilling, Enron revolutionized the energy market. The company pioneered strategies that allowed it to become a dominant player in an already saturated market and was celebrated for it. Business magazines, financial analysts, and other industry experts praised

Enron, giving it the title "America's Most Innovative Company" for six consecutive years from 1996 to 2001.

At the core of this success was an intense passion, verging on obsession for continuous growth, profit maximization, and complete market dominance. CEO Jeffrey Skilling personified this drive, this obsession, famously pushing his employees with slogans like "Ask why?" and "Think big." He purposefully fostered an intense corporate culture where extraordinary results weren't just celebrated—they were demanded. The executives had a relentless passion to increase stock prices and, ultimately, to impress Wall Street. This passion became obsessive, clouding their judgment and leading to risky decisions.

Enron's strategies drew admiration and envy from others. As Enron's executives pushed creative boundaries and experimented with new financial instruments, traded natural gas contracts, and eventually moved aggressively into electricity and broadband, they were being watched by the whole market. Their passion for profits was seemingly working, paying off spectacularly and attracting investors left, right, and center. Enron's stock price had inflated, just as planned. The executives quickly became intoxicated by their success, believing that the "visionary leadership" that had gotten them this far justified every new action and venture. This resulted in the overlooking of potential risks and ethical implications.

Beneath the surface, though, there was trouble brewing. As Enron's drive for profit intensified, the lack of rational caution and sound ethical judgment led to reckless and outright deceptive practices. Executives began to employ complex accounting schemes to conceal debts and artificially inflate earnings. The infamous "mark-to-market" accounting method allowed the company to book anticipated profits as immediate revenue, creating an illusion of perpetual growth. The passion for profit rapidly transformed into a desperation to sustain a facade, even at the expense of employees and transparency.

Enron employees who voiced concerns or questioned financial practices were immediately sidelined or pressured to remain silent. Internal auditors and whistleblowers were marginalized, and executives ignored any warnings they gave. External analysts who questioned Enron's opaque financial reports were publicly dismissed and portrayed as incapable of understanding Enron's new and "innovative" approach.

By late 2001, however, reality caught up with the company's deception. Financial analysts and investigative journalists uncovered alarming inconsistencies in the financial reports filed by Enron. Stock prices plummeted as investors panicked. Confidence in Enron as a brand and company quickly evaporated, causing Enron's carefully constructed empire of illusion to collapse dramatically.

This led to Enron filing for bankruptcy in December 2001, which sent shockwaves throughout global markets, destroying $60 billion in market value. Many Enron employees had invested their life savings in stock and had to sit and watch helplessly as their futures vanished overnight. Thousands lost jobs, pensions, and retirement funds and were plunged head-first into financial despair. Investors of all sizes faced devastating losses that ultimately shook public trust in "corporate America" right to its core.

The following legal battles revealed the horrific extent of Enron's unethical and fraudulent practices. Executives such as Jeffrey Skilling, Kenneth Lay, and Andrew Fastow faced indictments on charges ranging from fraud and conspiracy to insider trading. Two of the executives, Skilling and Fastow, were convicted and imprisoned. Kenneth Lay died before sentencing.

The catastrophic failure of Enron exposed what happens when passion for profit overshadows the principles of a business. Enron's spectacular rise and sudden demise are a powerful reminder of the consequences when passion takes hold, and rational judgment is left out of the equation.

The Enron scandal prompted much-needed regulatory reforms designed to prevent similar abuses in the future. This included the Sarbanes-Oxley Act, aiming to increase corporate governance transparency and accountability.

Enron's story could've been one of innovation, but passion turned to greed, has made it a cautionary tale instead. The tale warns leaders and organizations alike that unchecked passion inevitably leads to ruin, no matter how brilliant its successes may seem.

Case Study #6 - FTX – When Passion Drowns Prudence

Sam Bankman-Fried didn't appear to be a bad guy. Because he is too "brilliant" to care, he resembles the person who forgets to comb his hair and gets away with it. Initially, he appeared to be a charming oddball: wearing a hoodie, lacking sleep, playing video games during meetings, and consuming vegan fries while using a few keystrokes to transfer billions of dollars. A former Jane Street trader and MIT math whiz, Sam was motivated by a cause rather than caviar or yachts.

That cause was effective altruism, a philosophical movement that combines a hacker mentality with utilitarian ethics. The idea is to make as much money as you can so that you can donate it all. Some saw Sam as a hero of this new reasoning.

One day, he said, he would give $1 billion annually to organizations that prevented AI doomsday scenarios, fought pandemics, or saved lives.

Thus, he created FTX.

What began in 2019 as a cryptocurrency exchange swiftly grew into a titan. In less than three years, FTX rose to a $32 billion valuation thanks to the support of Silicon Valley elites, celebrity endorsements (Tom Brady, anyone?), and collaborations with lawmakers and regulators. In a lavish penthouse in the Bahamas, dedicated workers put in 12- to 18-hour days. It was all out of the ordinary. The leaders cohabitated, collaborated, and occasionally dated one another.

Behind it all was Sam, who was intense, idealistic, and becoming increasingly unbridled.

However, nobody understood that this empire, which was driven by passion, was based on quicksand until it was much too late. FTX had been transferring billions of customer deposits to Alameda Research, its sister hedge fund, to cover bad bets. A conflict of interest so blatant that it would have been flagged within days in any sane financial system. However, FTX exuded a sense of brilliance and mission that deterred criticism.

Sam's justification? He later asserted that it had nothing to do with greed. Maximizing impact was the goal. He wasn't only engaging in dangerous transactions. He was speeding up time and transforming the financial industry. He was building a war chest to save the world.

In one illuminating story, a worker expressed worries about the dangers of money transfers between FTX and Alameda. "We're smart enough to manage it," Sam allegedly responded. Arrogance had replaced passion. Conceit turned to delusion.

It all fell apart in November 2022. A startling concentration of assets in FTT—FTX's own exchange token—was revealed in an Alameda balance sheet leak. Trust vanished in a matter of days. A competitor exchange, Binance, openly withdrew from a bailout agreement. FTX declared bankruptcy. Clients' accounts were locked. Billions disappeared.

After being detained in the Bahamas, the cryptocurrency star was found guilty of fraud in the United States. At least in Sam's imagination, the dream of effective altruism turned into a warning about what happens when unbridled passion passes for reason rather than about evil.

The belief system that underpins FTX is just as tragic as the extent of the loss. He was the good guy, Sam believed. He had faith in the mission. However, belief turns dangerous if it is not supported by critical introspection. Without logic, passion can be both alluring and disastrous.

FTX was ultimately not a scam in the conventional sense. It was a self-consuming passion project. He began with good intentions and ended with handcuffs. And between? The methodical deterioration of caution, supervision, and common sense.

The collapse of FTX serves as a striking example of the perils of unbridled passion masquerading as morality. Sam Bankman-Fried was a bright, well-meaning idealist who allowed belief to transcend boundaries; he was not a cartoon villain. His tale illustrates how even the most brilliant minds can become blind to risk, responsibility, and reality due to passion, particularly when encased in a cause. Even the most selfless objectives become warped when reason is lacking. Prudence must temper passion, particularly when lives are at stake.

The FTX case study demonstrates that ego and emotion cannot be the compass in boardrooms, revolutions, or multibillion-dollar cryptocurrency empires. We'll sail straight into trouble if reason doesn't stay at the rudder.

Mastering Passion: Action Steps for Maintaining Reason

Passion can absolutely be a driving force behind success, but it must always be balanced with discipline and reason. Keeping passion in check requires conscious effort, self-awareness, and practical strategies that allow us to recognize emotional biases before they cloud our judgment.

One key tool for maintaining reason is embracing objective feedback. Passion often isolates people, driving us into echo chambers that confirm our emotional instincts. Proactively seeking external perspectives and inviting constructive criticism prevents passion from overwhelming our logic and reason.

Another tool is to practice emotional detachment. Using this tool when making critical decisions helps to prevent impulsive and reckless choices. Taking that moment to step back from a situation to analyze it objectively allows the mind to refocus and consider the logical and rational side of the debates. This can be crucial in preventing hasty mistakes.

Establishing rational boundaries is equally vital. Clearly defined limits protect against decisions driven solely by emotional intensity. Individuals and organizations can maintain control over passion by setting predetermined checkpoints, measurable criteria, and defined decision-making processes, preventing impulsivity and emotional blindness.

Choosing Reason Over Recklessness

Choosing reason over recklessness is crucial in making passion work for us rather than against us. It involves recognizing the dangers of unbridled passion and making intentional decisions that battle and tame our emotional impulses with logical thinking. Successful leaders and visionaries would never dream of discarding their passion. Instead, with careful practice, they harness it, using their rational thought to guide the emotional energy toward positive outcomes.

By embracing reason as the compass that guides our passionate pursuits, we can ensure that our decisions reflect thoughtful consideration and logical planning instead of emotional urgency alone.

Key Takeaways

1. Passion can inspire greatness or provoke catastrophe; control is crucial.

There's no denying that passion is a powerful, intense emotional fuel that can and does drive individuals and organizations toward extraordinary accomplishments. Passionate people have long propelled humanity forward, from groundbreaking scientific discoveries to cultural revolutions!

Passion inspired the Wright brothers to defy skeptics and achieve flight, and it fueled Martin Luther King Jr.'s relentless pursuit of civil rights. When passion is appropriately harnessed and used alongside rational thought, it catalyzes innovation and motivates us to push beyond preconceived limits and barriers, achieving the seemingly impossible.

The downfall comes with its intensity. Passion can quickly shift from beneficial to harmful if left unchecked. Its potential to inspire is equally likely to cause a catastrophe if it overrides reason. This is evident in the case of Napoleon Bonaparte—his intense passion for conquest and personal glory initially propelled him to victory. Still, as passion overtook his judgment, relentless ambition became an obsession, leading him to his biggest disaster.

Control is crucial in making sure passion is beneficial. Individuals who consciously manage and channel their emotional intensity are better positioned for sustained success. Think, for example, about

Steve Jobs. His passion for innovation famously fueled the success of Apple, but before that, his emotional intensity led to rash decisions, and he was ousted from the company. It wasn't until he learned to balance passion with reason that he transformed into the man we knew him to be until his passing.

2. Rational thinking must always guide emotional drive.

Emotional intensity and rational thinking are too often portrayed as mutually exclusive, with emotion pitted against logic as if the two were enemies. However, like passion, emotional drive can be a powerful motivator that provides the fuel needed for significant innovation and achievement. However, the key to harnessing this fuel is eliminating emotion and ensuring rational thought is used alongside passion, almost like its driving or guiding force. Rationality provides a perspective, a sense of clarity, and strategic direction that enables the channeling of emotional intensity into constructive decision-making and action.

However, when passion is allowed to operate independently of reason, it frequently leads to impulsive and ultimately detrimental decisions. The Challenger Space Shuttle disaster serves as a stark demonstration of this principle. The passion of NASA's management for space exploration and meeting already ambitious schedules overshadowed the rational safety warnings of experienced professionals. Emotionally driven urgency resulted in disregarding objective evidence, resulting in a tragedy that followed the company for many years to come. The disaster could've been avoided had reason been taken into consideration.

Some companies work as positive examples of this. Toyota, for example, demonstrates how passion and rationality can work together. Toyota is passionate about innovation, quality, and improvement, and those concepts are deeply embedded in its corporate culture. Their passion is always accompanied by methodical, reasoned decision-making, exemplified by their careful, evidence-driven approach to everything they do. As a result, Toyota has seen sustained success.

3. The greatest successes balance passion with reason.

History does a great job at demonstrating that the most remarkable achievements result from a delicate balance of passion and reason. With passion, we have a vision, but with reason, we have discipline, strategy, and clarity. Leaders and organizations must effectively find this balance to find sustainable success.

Think of Abraham Lincoln's presidency during the American Civil War. Lincoln's passion for justice, equality, and national unity was unmistakable, yet his decisions were always carefully reflected and made with explicit deliberation. He was passionate about abolishing slavery but only issued the Emancipation Proclamation after thoughtfully assessing the political, social, and military ramifications, which could be argued as the reason that his decision worked as well as it did. His careful balance between passion and reason secured his enduring legacy as one of history's most revered leaders.

In the world of business, Amazon is a prime example of the importance of balancing passion with reason. Jeff Bezos's passion for innovation, customer obsession, and long-term growth have fueled Amazon's rise from being an online bookstore to one of the world's largest corporations. The passion behind it all was always complemented by meticulous, data-driven decision-making. Bezos deliberately tests and learns about every product and decision they make, thus avoiding emotionally driven impulsiveness in favor of rational data analysis. This incredibly disciplined approach allowed Amazon to sustain such exponential growth without collapsing. This is just another prime example of how successful organizations can be when they balance passion with strategy.

It is clear that to achieve great success, there must be an intentional combination of passion and reason. Each element must complement and reinforce the other, providing equal parts energy and purpose and considering all of the rational ramifications of the decisions made.

4. Decisions made under intense emotional pressure should always be questioned and tempered with objective analysis.

Passionate feelings of urgency can significantly cloud judgment. Under these sorts of emotional pressures, people often feel they have to act quickly, and as a result, they make impulsive choices without carefully considering the consequences. Though usually well-intentioned, these decisions frequently ignore critical risks, leading to unintended and often detrimental outcomes. The importance of pausing to question emotionally driven choices cannot be overstated.

The financial collapse of Enron is a key example of failure to combat emotional pressure and reinforce it with objective analysis. Driven by an intense passion for growth and profit, Enron's leadership ignored clear warning signs, ethical guidelines, and logical business practices. Emotional pressure, rooted in passion and overwhelmed by irrational considerations, justifies unethical accounting practices. This unchecked emotional drive eventually led to one of the most infamous corporate downfalls in the country's history and devastated thousands.

In contrast, the heroic actions of Captain Chesley "Sully" Sullenberger during what came to be dubbed the "Miracle on the Hudson" were a complete success and only further prove the importance of combining our passion with rational thinking. Despite facing extreme stress and urgency when US Airways Flight 1549 lost both engines, Sullenburger analyzed all the options available and determined the best course of action. Rather than yielding to panic or impulse, he relied on rational decision-making and safely landed the plane on the Hudson River, saving all passengers and crew.

Clearly, leaders and decision-makers should do all in their power to cultivate the habit of questioning emotionally charged choices—even their own favor of employing structural analytical methods, seeking objective feedback, and rationally examining decisions.
Final Thoughts

Passion is a potent and celebrated force behind groundbreaking discoveries, heroic endeavors, and exceptional achievements, and rightly so. However, as vividly illustrated in the historical examples, passion without reason can lead swiftly and irreversibly to awful and even fatal consequences.

As discussed, Napoleon's ambition, once the foundation of his military genius and continental empire, quickly became his Achilles' heel during his Russian campaign. Driven by relentless ambition rather than any real strategy, he allowed emotional zeal to override his genius, and the result was his army facing catastrophic losses as they faced the reality of the brutal Russian terrain and climate. Ultimately, it signaled the downfall of Napoleon's empire. The tragedy tells us one thing: passion becomes destructive when divorced from rationality, no matter how powerful.

The tale of the Enron Corporation also demonstrates the devastating outcome when passion for profit eclipses rationality and ethics. Executives, led by Lay and Skilling, were committed to dominating the market. This drive soon morphed into an obsession that simply closed their eyes to constraints, financial policies, and rationality. As passion evolved into desperation, business practices gave way to fraudulent schemes that were designed to maintain a facade of success. Then, the truth emerged, and the fallout was truly awful. Their mistake illustrates that unchecked passion can lead to appalling consequences.

Likewise, the Challenger disaster serves as another profound cautionary tale, this time with fatal consequences. NASA's passion for space exploration, innovation, and its own public image overshadowed critical safety considerations and rational judgment. Explicit warnings from engineers were ignored, and the result was a tragedy broadcast live worldwide, forever etched into the memory of thousands who watched live as people were lost forever.

Each one of these historical examples vividly illustrates a consistent pattern: passion can be inspirational, but it can also be devastating. Depending on what it is anchored to, passion can motivate creativity and innovation and lead us to catastrophe.

Mastering passion involves deliberate self-awareness and effort. Leaders, individuals, and even organizations must be able to take that all-important step back, reflect critically, and carefully evaluate whether their enthusiasm is leading their decisions. They must reflect critically on their thoughts and plans and ensure that all they do aligns with sound judgment, relevant ethical standards, and risk assessments. To successfully master passion, we must recognize the subtle indicators of obsession and unhealthy enthusiasm, such as impatience, refusal to acknowledge objections, disregard for contrary evidence or opinion, and unwillingness to pause.

The goal should never be to suppress passion but to balance it. When balanced, we can use passion as the driving force behind innovation, success, and growth, and we can prevent it from spiraling and causing those historically destructive outcomes.

To harness passion and to better understand and tackle the enemy within, consider these guiding principles:

- Passion can fuel unprecedented success or unprecedented failure — the direction it goes depends on how well-disciplined the individual is.

- Rational decision-making and logical thinking must always guide passionate endeavors.

- Sustainable success comes from balancing emotional intensity with objective analysis.

- Decisions that are driven solely by emotional pressure must be re-evaluated and reconsidered.

As you reflect on these powerful lessons from across modern and ancient history, ask yourself: is your passion serving your goals, or have you become a slave to emotional intensity?

You may be surprised at your answer. Hopefully, you'll find that your answer will influence your personal and professional trajectory and profoundly shape your life and the legacy you leave. Passion unbridled leaves a trail of destruction; passion tamed creates lasting success. The choice—and the consequences thereafter—is yours to make.

CHAPTER 3
PRIDE IS THE ENEMY OF FRIENDSHIP

"Pride is concerned with who is right. Humility is concerned with what is right." — Ezra Taft Benson.

Understanding Pride and Its Hidden Danger

Often mistaken for self-esteem or confidence, pride involves one's perceived superiority over others. It is a social trait that can solidify relationships through mutual admiration, but that can just as quickly spiral into an obstacle, creating barriers rather than connections.

Pride's distinctive feature is its external focus. It doesn't inflate one's self-worth; instead, it actively diminishes the value of others. It makes individuals reluctant to see their errors, apologize, and even acknowledge the validity of others' viewpoints. It's almost like a social competitiveness, an obsession with being right instead of doing what's right. This can, if left unchecked, slowly destroy relationships from within.

The Cost of Pride-Drive Decisions – Real-World Case Studies

Pride can quietly transform what should be minor disagreements into deep, relationship-ending rifts. It is the silent killer of all sorts of relationships and can even lead to people prioritizing their point over preserving the relationship itself. It can prevent genuine apologies and cause resentment to build over time.

Pride convinces us that winning an argument is more important than curating and sustaining trust, empathy, and understanding.

Case Study #7 - Nikola Tesla and Thomas Edison: A Rivalry Fueled by Pride

In the late nineteenth century, America stood at the start of what would come to be a remarkable technological revolution. At the core of it were two extraordinary minds: Nikola Tesla and Thomas Edison.

The two men initially had a promising relationship and fostered a connection built on mutual admiration and respect. Tesla was a brilliant young inventor from Serbia who had arrived in the United States in 1884 with nothing but an introduction letter addressed to Edison, who had already cemented himself as a renowned American inventor.

Edison welcomed Tesla into his laboratory, intrigued by the young man's talent and potential. It wasn't long, however, before seeds of rivalry sprouted. Edison was famously tenacious and proud and had battled skeptics for years before securing his reputation as America's foremost inventor. On the other hand, Tesla was a genius with innovative ideas far ahead of his time.

Their first pride-driven conflict surfaced over the debate surrounding electrical currents: Edison's direct current (DC) versus Tesla's alternating current (AC). Edison had heavily invested both financially and emotionally in DC technology. He proudly and stubbornly dismissed Tesla's ideas as dangerous and outright impractical. However, his pride was bruised when Tesla demonstrated that AC could transmit electricity over a much larger distance than DC technology.

Rather than recognizing Tesla's advancements as valuable innovations, Edison reacted defensively, intensifying a pride-based rivalry that would become legendary.

The situation worsened when Edison refused to honor an allegedly promised bonus for Tesla's work improving his DC generators. Tesla, feeling betrayed, left Edison's company. He was bitter and determined to prove himself independently. Soon, pride fueled both inventors, turning their once mutual admiration into intense competition. Edison was unwilling to admit any flaw or shortcoming and publicly attacked Tesla's work, launching outright aggressive campaigns that set out to undermine AC technology. The goal? To remove any interest investors or the public might have.

At one point, Edison arranged public electrocution of animals, even executing an elephant named Topsy at Luna Park. The idea was to portray AC as inherently deadly. He was driven by pure pride and the determination to maintain dominance. He relied heavily on fear-mongering rather than honest competition, which deepened the two men's personal animosity.

In response, fueled by wounded pride, Tesla became increasingly isolated and obsessive. Rather than diplomatically engaging Edison or strategically collaborating with other inventors, Tesla pursued his visions independently, often at the cost of practicality and financial security. Ultimately, this cost him opportunities for greater recognition and the finances he so desperately needed.

The conflict between the two men significantly impacted the technological process. Their pride prevented what could've been one of the greatest collaborative relationships in the history of science. Had Edison embraced humility, he and Tesla could've unified their genius, revolutionizing energy and accelerating America's electrical revolution. Likewise, had Tesla tempered his pride for long enough to maintain a constructive conversation, he might have

Their rivalry is a prime example of the devastating consequences of unchecked pride. What had been mutual respect and a desire for collaboration quickly became a barrier instead, limiting their potential and delaying any technological advancement they could've had together.

Tesa died impoverished and, in the end, relatively unknown. His genius was only fully appreciated posthumously. On the other hand, Edison left behind a mixed legacy tainted by his behavior toward Tesla.

Now, we look back at the Tesla-Edison conflict as a powerful reminder of pride's destructive qualities. It destroyed their relationship and completely squandered the extraordinary possibilities of their cooperation. It is a timeless lesson about how humility, mutual respect, and recognizing others' abilities can bridge divides. Pride, on the other hand, builds walls, isolates people, and inevitably diminishes our possibilities as people.

The historic rivalry between Tesla and Edison illustrates one thing: true greatness is not simply about individual brilliance, but also collaboration. Tesla and Edison could've both gone and done much more in their lives had they worked together, but instead, one died a pauper, and the other smeared his reputation through the dirt. By accepting pride over collaboration and learning from others, we risk limiting ourselves and stagnating, just like they did.

Case Study #8 - Steve Jobs and Steve Wozniak: A Friendship Fractured by Pride

The story of Steve Jobs and Steve Wozniak is legendary. It is a tale of two friends who revolutionized the tech world by creating Apple, a company destined to reshape society as they knew it. Their complementary skills and their genuine friendship initially fueled their partnership. Jobs was a charismatic man with a vision and a keen eye for aesthetics, user experience, and marketing. Alternatively, Woznkiak was a technical genius who was celebrated for his exceptional skills and creativity.

Their partnership started in the 1970s in a garage in Silicon Valley. With plenty of youthful enthusiasm and a shared passion for technology, they created Apple I and Apple II, revolutionary projects that propelled the name Apple into global prominence and kick-started the personal computing trend.

But, as Apple transformed into an iconic international brand, pride began subtly infiltrating their relationship. Steve Jobs's pride was growing day by day. Tied to his relentless pursuit of public recognition and perfection, it developed as the business did until he began to see himself as Apple's singular visionary. He started to overlook and minimize his friend's contributions. Soon enough, public appearances, media interactions, and everything public-facing increasingly highlighted Jobs over Wozniak. Wozniak's profound technical abilities went uncelebrated as he quietly continued to work tirelessly in the shadows.

This led to Wozniak feeling undervalued, and despite his genuine affection for his friend, he felt marginalized. His groundbreaking technological achievements were often credited solely to Jobs, and pride was stopping Jobs from publicly acknowledging Wozniak, instead nurturing his image as Apple's sole driving

During the launch of Apple II, which Wozniak's engineering brilliance was to thank for, Jobs allowed himself to dominate all media coverage completely. He took the interviews, and he was in all promo materials. Even internally, he decided to take more control and seek more recognition, which only fuelled tension and resentment in Wozniak. Pride, now a part of Jobs' self, prevented him from realizing how much acknowledgment he stole from his friend.

After being pushed further and further to the side, Wozniak eventually had enough. In 1985, he left Apple to pursue independent projects and participate in philanthropic projects aligned more with his values. The departure was quiet, but its impact was profound, and it marked an obvious end of a remarkable professional collaboration and a years-long friendship.

Many years later, reflecting on what happened, Steve Jobs said he regretted how pride had clouded his judgment and behavior—but the damage was irreparable. Their friendship could never be fully restored. Pride had left its footprint, placing a permanent divide between Wozniak and Jobs and their work.

The story of this fractured friendship is a powerful cautionary tale demonstrating pride's destructive capacity. Had Jobs publicly celebrated and valued his friend's critical role in the development of Apple, their collaboration could have thrived. They could have created an even stronger, more innovative brand. Instead, Jobs' relentless pride and his pursuit of personal glory undermined personal bonds, hindering the possibility of an inclusive, collaborative corporate culture.

Looking at Jobs and Wozniak, we can see how pride can silently corrode even the strongest partnerships. Their story is a testament to the need for humility, open communication, acknowledgment, genuine appreciation, and respect within professional and personal relationships.

Steve Jobs is now remembered as an iconic figure, but his legacy is tainted by an awareness of the high price he paid for pride. Alternatively, Wozniak is less publicly recognized, but he is widely honored within the technology community for his humility, integrity, and contributions to the sector.

The friendship and subsequent estrangement of these two geniuses highlight the delicate balance required between ambition and humility. It shines a light on how pride fractures bonds and isolates even the most innovative people, diminishing collective potential. Working with humility, on the other hand, can foster long-term, lasting friendships and collaborative efforts, enhancing our legacies.

Case Study #9 - The Beatles: A Legendary Band Torn Apart by Pride

The Beatles, arguably the most influential bands in musical history, redefined music, culture, and popular entertainment. John Lennon, Paul McCartney, George Arrison and Ringo Starr began their journey as close friends. Their bond seemed unbreakable in the early years as they started in the clubs of Liverpool and Hamburg.

When the band started, John Lennon and Paul McCartney's friendship kept them together. They had an unmatched synergy. Their creative partnership was responsible for "Hey Jude," "Yesterday", and "A Day in the Life". The songs were almost instant classics, catapulting The Beatles into the stratosphere, where they would remain for the rest of their career.

In their early days, their friendship was pivotal to the band's success, and yet, beneath the collective genius, seeds of pride were being sewn. As The Beatles' fame grew worldwide, Lennon and McCartney started to view each other as competitors, driven by pride and desires to assert their individual superiority and artistic dominance. The camaraderie they once shared started to give way to tensions.

The turning point came during the band's creative process for "The White Album" in 1968. Lennon and McCartney reportedly clashed frequently in the studio over their devotion to their artistic visions. Their prideful insistence on their ideas led to arguments over almost every facet of the creative process. What had been a dynamic partnership became increasingly strained by the insistence from each of them that their ideas were better.

George Harrison and Ringo Starr, caught on the battlefield, experienced growing frustrations. Harrison, a gifted songwriter, found his contributions were frequently being overlooked and ignored in favor of the others' works. Meanwhile, Starr, often the mediator, struggled to maintain any unity amidst the escalating arguments. Pride had started to fracture friendships and undermine the collaborative connection the band once had.

It went beyond creative tensions, though. The Beatles faced escalating conflicts over business and management-related decisions. Lennon appointed manager Allen Klein, despite McCartney explicitly objecting, which only escalated pride-driven confrontations. McCartney viewed Klein's appointment as undermining his autonomy, which amplified resentment between them. Lennon, convinced of his correctness, refused to compromise, emphasizing the growing chasm between the two of them.

Personal differences only deepened the rift. Lennon's relationship with Yoko Ono introduced tension as her presence disrupted the band dynamics. McCartney, Starr, and Harrison felt bothered as Lennon's pride prevented him from acknowledging their concerns as legitimate. Prideful stubbornness once again replaced any open dialogue, fostering an environment marked by bitterness and isolation.

By 1970, pride had completely fractured the friendships at the heart of The Beatles. Lennon and McCartney, whose partnership once fueled creative brilliance, barely talked. Their relationship was overshadowed by resentment and pride. Eventually, it became too much, and the band broke up, shocking the world and highlighting pride's devastating consequences, eclipsing friendship, trust, and humility.

Long after the band's breakup, both Lennon and McCartney expressed regret for allowing their pride and competitive natures to dominate their interactions. The two men recognized, years too late, the extraordinary potential lost in their refusal to work together and to prioritize friendship and collaboration over pride.

Their unparalleled partnership could have continued if they embraced humility and set aside that pride. Their humility could have fostered sustainable innovation, creative evolution, and a strong platonic connection. Instead, they allowed pride to destroy a legendary partnership, robbing the world of even more musical innovation.

The story of The Beatles is a vivid illustration of pride's hidden ganger. Though subtle, pride silently chips away at crucial relationships, diminishing the potential we share as a collective. Lennon and McCartney's partnership, initially built on mutual admiration and true friendship, was tragically eroded by pride and ruined by their subsequent unwillingness to acknowledge one another's worth.

The Beatles' legacy can be seen in their remarkable music and as a poignant reminder of the destruction pride can leave in its wake. Had humility prevailed over pride, their partnership, friendship, and even the band might have flourished for decades longer.

Unfortunately, that wasn't the case. Instead, the Beatles remain a key example of a critical truth: relationships thrive when pride gives way to humility.

Mastering Pride: Action Steps for Preserving Relationships

Pride doesn't have to sabotage our relationships. We can master pride, but it requires humility and a sincere willingness to prioritize those relationships over our personal validation. We must make a conscious effort and focus on empathy, effort, and self-awareness.

When a disagreement arises, we must recognize when pride is inhibiting reconciliation. Apologizing sincerely, without a justification or excuse, signals strength, and it is these sorts of apologies that allow us to rebuild trust and foster deeper bonds that promote respect and humility.

We must also be able to listen openly without becoming defensive—this is a key step to preserving relationships and protecting our connections from pride. Active listening validates others' perspectives and reduces the harmful effects that pride might have.

Another way to overcome pride is to acknowledge personal fallibility. Humbly accepting our mistakes allows us to learn from them and grow. Recognizing our failures can improve our judgment and strengthen our bonds.

Expressing genuine appreciation will also ensure that relationships remain vibrant. When pride tempts us to see our friends as rivals, appreciation focuses on their value and why we love and appreciate them rather than on their value to our lives. Celebrating others' and their successes allows us to build stronger bonds rather than feeding envy or competition.

Key Takeaways - Choosing Humility over Pride

Pride creates barriers, while humility fosters connection.

If we let it, pride erect walls in relationships. It makes communication difficult and forgiveness near impossible. Humility, however, opens doors for dialogue, understanding, and reconciliation. Great leaders have long understood this and have made efforts. One example is Nelson Mandela, who set aside personal pride to build and maintain connections.

Friendships are sustained through openness, not self-righteousness.

Pride forces us to prove ourselves right, whereas humility asks us what is right, strengthening friendships through mutual respect. The Beatles' dissolution highlights that we destroy unity when we insist on personal superiority. But if we focus and collaborate, we can build enduring bonds. Successful teams and relationships prioritize the latter, focusing on collective purpose rather than individual accolades.

True strength lies in admitting faults and seeking reconciliation.

Admitting fault or admitting our mistakes takes courage and is an act of strength. Historical friendships, such as the bond between Thomas Jefferson and John Adams, US founders, survived because both parties could recognize their faults. In contrast, Tesla and Edison missed this opportunity, overwhelmed by their individual pride.

Final Thoughts

Though often overlooked, pride is the destroyer of bonds. The stories of Nikola Tesla and Thomas Edison, Steve Jobs and Steve Wozniak, John Lennon, and Paul McCartney offer invaluable insight into pride's destructive power. Each historic pair began as partners whose combined creativity and friendship generated groundbreaking achievements that shaped history. Unfortunately, pride gradually infiltrated their relationships, bitterly twisting them away from one another and transforming what was once synergy and friendship into bitterness.

The rivalry between Tesla and Edison epitomizes exactly how pride can poison potential. Two extraordinary inventors who could've propelled humanity forward, achieving technological advancements beyond what each of them could've done independently. Instead, pride took them down a path of relentless competition and animosity.

The narrative of Jobs and Wozniak also highlights how pride can fracture even the strongest of friendships. Once united by a shared passion and friendship, their relationship strained when pride got involved. While Apple continued to survive, their friendship did not. The loss was profound for both of them.

The Beatles' dissolution, arguably the most culturally impactful example, demonstrates pride's capacity to destroy even legendary collaborations and relationships. John Lennon and Paul McCartney, once considered inseparable creative forces, allowed pride to pit them against one another rather than fuel their ambition as a creative unit. Prideful insistence on individual superiority ate away at the empathy and communication within the group until there was little to no mutual respect, and the band had no choice but to break up, leaving the world deprived of future music from a legendary group and bitterness with both men.

These historical examples reinforce what we know to be true: pride sabotages relationships by forcing individuals to prioritize personal validation over collective growth. It encourages people to pursue short-term personal victories at the expense of lasting bonds, creating resentment and malice long after the initial conflict fades.

Mastering our pride requires continuous, deliberate effort. It requires us to be self-aware, emotionally intelligent, and willing to prioritize our relationships. We must be willing to accept that true strength is in humility, admitting mistakes, accepting criticism, and acknowledging the worth of others. People who master pride can create more substantial, enduring bonds, enabling more outstanding collective achievements than those who isolate themselves through prideful behavior.

Looking back through history, examples of great reconciliation, like that of Thomas Jefferson and John Adams, show us that humility is powerful enough to restore even severely fractured relationships. These tales of reconciliation tell us that humility is capable of much more than pride—it can strengthen bonds, heal wounds, and rebuild more substantial connections.

Consider these historical lessons and the profound implications these examples might have on your relationships and legacy. Remember that pride may offer short-term satisfaction but will inevitably result in long-term isolation and hurt. Instead, favor humility, which creates genuine, enduring connections.

Pride is not some inevitable force. It is a conscious choice we must reject to sustain meaningful relationships. Humility over pride is essential for personal fulfillment, professional success, and sustainable happiness.

It is time to ask yourself honestly: are you choosing pride or humility in your interactions?

Whatever your answer, it will shape your friendships,

CHAPTER 4: RATIONALIZATION IS THE ENEMY OF INTEGRITY

"The greatest way to live with honor in this world is to be what we pretend to be." — Socrates.

Integrity is the foundation of trust, ethics, and strong leadership. However, when people start to rationalize their actions, they begin to erode their moral compass. The erosion of morals makes it easier to ignore integrity and justify ethical breaches. Rationalization, in essence, allows people to excuse behavior that they know is wrong by convincing themselves that their actions are, in fact, necessary, justified, or harmless. This can lead to many scandals, and it has done so throughout history.

Understanding Rationalization and the Subtle Erosion of Integrity

At its core, rationalization is a psychological defense mechanism that allows individuals to justify behaviors or decisions considered morally or ethically questionable. This process often involves creating plausible but inaccurate explanations to reinforce a positive self-image or reduce discomfort caused by the cognitive dissonance that occurs when we make choices we know are wrong. Rationalization is the mind's attempt to align actions with values, even when the actions do not align. We must understand this concept as individuals, as the process quietly wears away our integrity and, if left unchecked, can blur the lines between right and wrong.

A key part of rationalization is its subtlety. Like many of the seven traits discussed in this book, rationalization can often masquerade as something else. In this case, it often masquerades as reason, logic, or even practicality. Individuals will frequently convince themselves entirely that their choices are justified based on their unique circumstances, exceptional needs, or perceived pressures. For example, they might rationalize unethical workplace behavior by pointing to stress or unfair treatment from management. These justifications, while seemingly reasonable initially, will usually lead to a slippery slope of declining standards of integrity.

This behavior thrives in environments that lack clear ethical boundaries or structures of accountability. When ethical expectations are vague or inconsistently enforced, people are more likely to rationalize behavior that might usually be considered unacceptable. Ambiguity encourages rationalization, and in contexts rife with ambiguity and uncertainty, people can convince themselves that their actions are permissible or, in some circumstances, even necessary. This only goes to highlight the necessity of explicit ethical standards and accountability.

Rationalization's destruction is particularly malicious because it is self-reinforcing. Every instance of justified misconduct lowers a person's moral threshold, making future rationalizations easier to commit. What starts as small compromises evolve into significant ethical failings can soon evolve into significant ethical failings. Over time, this repetitive cycle creates a habitual pattern of behavior that significantly damages a person's character.

Trying to combat rationalization requires self-awareness and a firm commitment to personal honesty. We must actively question our motives, decisions, and even the explanations we provide in response—especially in ethically ambiguous situations. Cultivating a personal, professional, or social environment that openly challenges rationalizations and promotes a transparent and ethical dialogue can significantly lessen the risk of rationalization.

The Slippery Slope of Justifying Wrongdoing

Case Study #10 – Theranos: When Ambition Undermined Integrity

Elizabeth Holmes founded Theranos in 2003 and promised to

revolutionize healthcare through groundbreaking blood-testing technology. Holmes was a charismatic and compelling woman who captured global attention with her vision of comprehensive diagnostic tests from a single drop of blood. Investors poured billions into Theranos, quickly taking her startup to a multi-billion-dollar business.

Elizabeth Holmes was hailed as a visionary and an entrepreneur like no other, and she was compared to other big tech giants like Steve Jobs. She very quickly became America's youngest self-made female billionaire. People liked her; her passion lay in making healthcare accessible, and that resonated with people up and down the country. It attracted high-profile investors, prominent board members, and extensive media coverage. At its peak, Theranos represented the very type of innovation that had made Silicone Valley famous.

However, beneath the narrative shown to the media, there was a disconnect between Theranos's claims and reality. The revolutionary tech that Holmes had passionately made her billions on, known as the Edison device, was incapable of reliably performing the broad range of blood tests it promised. Engineers and lab technicians internally raised concerns about the limits of the device, the inaccuracies in its reports, and the testing failures, but their warnings were cast aside—or, in some cases, actively suppressed.

Holmes and her associate, Ramesh "Sunny" Balwani, quickly began rationalizing their actions. They chose secrecy rather than being honest and acknowledging the technological setbacks they'd encountered. Holmes knowingly misled investors, regulators, and the public about the capabilities of her device. Rationalization was used to back these decisions up. They convinced themselves that the inaccuracies were just initial setbacks and that breakthroughs were imminent, so it was okay to hide the truth, as it would only be for a while.

These rationalizations escalated. Theranos increasingly had to lie on secrecy, internal intimidation, and even deceptive practices to maintain the appearance they'd created. Holmes and Balwani presented falsified demonstrations to investors and regulators, claiming the technology was completely functional. What was really happening, though, was the results were being provided by traditional, commercially available blood test machines. Employees who were aware of the deception tried to raise ethical concerns but were silenced and threatened with legal action.

This culture of rationalized secrecy created a self-perpetuating cycle. Every new compromise justified further deception, with Holmes and her leadership team convincing themselves that they were preserving their vision until technology caught up. The public accolades and investor confidence kept them going, blinding them to their unethical behavior's catastrophic risks and dangers.

The eventual exposure of Theranos came through a persistent journalist investigation, notably by John Carreyrou of The Wall Street Journal. He reported that Theranos's technology never worked as advertised and revealed that they hid a vast and complex fraud case. The result was Theranos collapsing spectacularly, with its valuation plummeting from $9 billion to almost nothing pretty much overnight.

Holmes and Balwani both faced criminal fraud charges that permanently damaged their reputations. Investors in the company lost millions, and employees lost their jobs and careers. Patients who had trusted Theranos's tests faced health risks due to inaccurate results.

The Theranos scandal illustrates how unchecked ambition and rationalization can undermine even the most promising and wholesome ventures. Had Holmes demonstrated the courage and integrity to admit technological failures, she might have been able to salvage Theranos's vision through honest collaboration and innovation rather than deception.

Ultimately, integrity is not just an ethical ideal. It is a practical necessity for sustained success. Holmes and the fall of Theranos is a sobering reminder that ambition without any integrity is not sustainable. Innovation and achievement must rely on transparency, accountability, and a genuine commitment to ethical practices.

The story of Theranos is also a critical lesson to entrepreneurs, leaders, and organizations, demonstrating that integrity must guide ambition and innovation, not the other way around. Leaders who value integrity create enduring legacies.

Ultimately, Theranos's downfall shows us that integrity is non-negotiable. Ambition without honesty inevitably leads to ruin, while integrity ensures lasting achievement and respect.

Case Study #11 – Lance Armstrong: A Career Tainted by Rationalization

Once regarded as an iconic symbol of resilience, Lance Armstrong was seen as the peak of determination and athletic excellence. After what was deemed a remarkable recovery from life-threatening testicular cancer, he captured global admiration when he won seven consecutive Tour de France titles from 1999 to 2005, which had never been done before. His victories made him not only a sports legend but a beacon of hope and inspiration for millions worldwide.

Armstrong wasn't just successful in cycling. He quickly became a powerful global brand, founding the Livestrong Foundation, that raised millions for cancer research. Armstrong's Livestrong movement inspired cancer survivors worldwide, further solidifying his status as an international hero whose perseverance against overwhelming odds was an inspiration for all.

However, hidden beneath Armstrong's celebrated image was a disturbing reality he had denied for years. Armstrong had been engaged in one of the most sophisticated and widespread doping operations in sports history. Armstrong initially rationalized his decision to use performance-enhancing drugs by convincing himself that he was leveling the playing field. At that point in time, cycling as a sport had become notoriously plagued by doping, so Armstrong convinced himself it was a necessary evil to respond to the competition and widespread corruption surrounding the sport. In his eyes, it was a pragmatic strategy, not an ethical violation.

Armstrong's rationalizations grew increasingly complicated. Fueled by pride and the intense pressure to maintain his unprecedented winning streak and global image. He argued internally, and, after his secrets were out, publicly, that doping merely balanced the scales since many of his rivals were doping too. This self-justification allowed him to sidestep personal accountability.

Over the years, Armstrong had gone to extraordinary lengths to sustain his deception. He'd aggressively silenced critics with lawsuits, intimidation, and character assassination against anyone who dared to come near. Armstrong sued journalists who published doping allegations and utilized his enormous influence wherever possible to discredit whistleblowers.

Numerous investigations occurred, but Armstrong's vehement denials sustained his image and falsified integrity for some time. His influence and reputation allowed him to dismiss critics. He rationalized that protecting his reputation was vital for himself and the broader message of hope he had come to stand for.

These rationalizations eventually collapsed under overwhelming evidence in 2012. The United States Anti-Doping Agency (USADA) published a detailed report detailing Armstrong's systematic doping practices. The report was undeniable. It included testimonies from former teammates and associates who could describe in detail all of Armstrong's aggressive intimidation tactics, doping methods, and deliberate deception.

When faced with indisputable evidence, Armstrong's defiance finally ended. In a high-profile interview with Oprah Winfrey in January 2013, Armstrong publicly admitted to doping throughout his career. The confession sent shockwaves across the sports world and beyond. The International Cycling Union stripped him of all of his Tour de France titles and banned him for life from professional cycling. His sponsors quickly abandoned him as his once-celebrated reputation was shattered irreparably.

The aftermath of his confession was not just a personal one. It casts a long shadow over cycling and sports ethics as a whole. Armstrong's rationalizations compromised his integrity and damaged the trust of millions who believed in his inspirational narrative of resilience and perseverance. Armstrong later admitted that he understood the devastating impact of his choices and expressed regret for the damage inflicted upon his fans, friends, and fellow competitors.

Had Armstrong decided to confront his ethical dilemmas honestly and chosen integrity over rationalization, his legacy may have remained a powerful symbol of resilience. Instead, he became a cautionary tale about the destructive potential of rationalizing unethical behavior. Armstrong's story illustrates that integrity is indispensable, even under pressure to succeed.

The lesson that Lance Armstrong left in his wake is clear and compelling: integrity is the foundation upon which all lasting success is constructed. No matter how justified it may initially seem, rationalization inevitably leads to ruin. Sustained success and genuine respect come only from maintaining consistent integrity, even if it demands personal sacrifice and courage.

Armstrong's tragic fall from grace reminds leaders, individuals, and athletes everywhere that true greatness is built upon integrity, not upon victories achieved at the cost of personal values.

Case Study #12 – Volkswagen Emissions Scandal: Corporate Deception Justified by Business Goals

In the early 2010s, Volkswagen aspired to dominate the global automotive industry. It started aggressively marketing its diesel vehicles as eco-friendly and fuel-efficient. This ambitious goal came with substantial pressure to meet tight emission standards, particularly in the United States, where environmental regulations were getting increasingly rigorous. Rather than embracing genuine innovation or exciting technological advancements to achieve these standards, Volkswagen executives made a disastrous decision rooted in corporate rationalization.

Volkswagen installed deceptive software, famously known as a "defeat device," in millions of diesel vehicles. This software detected when vehicles were undergoing emissions testing and activated emission controls specifically during those times. However, under normal driving conditions, the cars emitted pollutants up to 40 times above the allowable limits, significantly contributing to environmental harm and undermining public trust.

Volkswagen executives rationalized this unethical decision by over-emphasizing fierce competition in the industry. They convinced themselves that it was far too costly to try and meet emission standards and that doing so would compromise market share and profitability. They even went as far as to argue that customers cared more about fuel efficiency, performance, and price, not emissions compliance. This rationalized their decisions and allowed them to overlook their deceptive practices.

The deception went undetected for years, allowing Volkswagen to boast "remarkable growth" and consumer confidence. The cars sold exceptionally well, bolstered by aggressive marketing around "clean diesel" technology. Executives maintained their rationalization, convincing themselves it was harmless and merely a temporary strategy to maintain competitiveness until genuine technological improvements could be developed.

In September 2015, Volkwagen's carefully constructed facade was utterly unraveled. The United States Environmental Protection Agency (EPA) discovered the fraudulent practices. The revelation completely shook the automotive industry and consumers worldwide. It escalated into an international scandal, severely damaging the company's credibility and brand reputation.

The consequences of the truth were immediate and severe. Volkswagen faced unprecedented financial penalties that totaled billions of dollars across the globe. Legal actions piled up rapidly, and customers filed consumers, as did environmental agencies and governmental authorities across multiple nations. Volkswagen also experienced a severe erosion of consumer trust, tarnishing a decades-long reputation as a reliable brand.

The scandal led to significant leadership upheaval, with key executives, including CEO Martin Winterkorn, resigning or facing criminal investigations. The crisis forced Volkswagen to undergo a costly restructuring and rebranding effort, which took billions from the innovation and growth of the company, redirecting it toward fines, settlements, and PR damage control.

Had the Volkswagen executives prioritized real innovation and integrity over profit and competition, the company could have developed legitimate technological solutions that met environmental standards. By choosing deception over innovation, Volkswagen compromised its integrity and, as a result, forfeited long-term credibility and consumer loyalty.

This scandal remains one of modern business history's most infamous examples of corporate rationalization. It highlights the consequences that occur when integrity is compromised for short-term gains. Volkswagen's story is a potent reminder that integrity cannot be exchanged for business success. Ethical conduct, transparency, and genuine innovation are far more reliable pathways to achieving sustainable profitability and brand strength.

The Volkswagen scandal underscored that authentic corporate leadership demands an unwavering commitment to ethics, integrity, and honesty, even amid intense market competition.

Mastering Integrity: Confronting and Overcoming Rationalization

In moments of intense pressure or temptation, integrity is frequently tested. Rationalization often emerges subtly in these moments. It provides comfort and justification for actions we know to be wrong. Mastering integrity involves consciously confronting and overcoming that comfort. Integrity isn't just sticking to external and internal rules; it involves rigorous self-examination, self-awareness, and consistent judgment, even when inconvenient.

The first crucial step toward mastering integrity is recognizing when rationalization is occurring. Rationalization is sneaky; it often hides, masking itself as practicality, urgency, or necessity. When tempted by what may seem like harmless ethical compromises, we must pause and ask ourselves critical questions. Would you openly defend this decision to the public? Would you confidently explain the decision to someone whose opinion you deeply respect? By reflecting on these questions, we can find clarity and reveal the subtle moral compromises to which rationalizations subject us.

In addition to self-awareness, we must seek external accountability. Trusted mentors, colleagues, or ethical advisors can provide invaluable perspectives that challenge rationalizations. This can help us to maintain moral clarity. External accountability encourages proper transparent discussion, cultivating a culture where integrity can thrive.

Transparency also plays a pivotal role in sustaining integrity. Individuals and organizations committed to transparency communicate their decisions openly, making unethical choices less viable. Transparency invites scrutiny and feedback, which are key to maintaining moral clarity reducing opportunities for unethical rationalization to take root.

Learning from our past ethical failures is also crucial when avoiding rationalization. Reflecting honestly and sincerely can help us to acknowledge when ethical compromises have occurred and thus allow us to prevent them from happening again. Committing to this genuine reflection helps us to grow and understand our moral standards to a better degree, which will inform future ethical decisions.

To master integrity, we must continuously choose long-term ethical considerations over temporary conveniences. Integrity, in essence, represents sustained moral courage and the ability to prioritize what is ethically correct consistently.

Key Takeaways

- Rationalization undermines ethical decision-making and can escalate rapidly, causing significant damage.
- Ethical leadership demands proactive accountability, transparency, and openness to external perspectives.
- Integrity requires consistent self-awareness, rigorous self-examination, and a commitment to continuous ethical growth.
- Prioritizing integrity fosters trust, credibility, and sustainable long-term success.

Final Thoughts: Integrity

Integrity is easily one of the most valuable assets any individual or organization can have. It is pivotal to ethical conduct and trust, respect, and long-term success. It's the cornerstone that solid relationships, lasting success, and believable leadership are constructed. Integrity isn't an abstract ideal nor a passive attribute; it takes consistent attention, self-awareness, and moral courage.

Some historical examples show us what happens when we allow integrity to falter. The rise and spectacular fall of Theranos, Lance Armstrong's tarnished legacy, and even the global fallout of the Volkswagen scandal all serve as reminders of how important integrity is in ensuring sustainable success. In each story, it is clear that seemingly minor ethical concessions escalate and continue to build until they inevitably avalanche into catastrophe.

Integrity flourishes not when tested in convenient situations but when the most severe ethical dilemmas occur. Leaders such as Abraham Lincoln and Nelson Mandela illustrate the lasting influence of integrity. Both preferred steadfast ethical values to convenience, personal ambition, or popularity, and they left lasting legacies characterized by moral courage and true leadership.

In situations where integrity is lost, it is hard, if not impossible, to regain it. Trust lost due to ethical compromise takes years to rebuild and, at times, is forever lost. Companies like Volkswagen discovered this fact first-hand, and individuals like Armstrong learned quickly that their reputations can never be untarnished.

This is why we must strive to maintain integrity. It is achievable and gratifying. Companies like Patagonia and leaders like Warren Buffet clearly demonstrate that living and working with unwavering integrity fosters a degree of trust, which is key to sustained success. These leaders' steadfast commitment to ethical transparency and to being held accountable allows them to maintain stellar reputations that inspire respect and ensure success.

Ultimately, integrity is not about adhering to ethical principles but about embodying those principles. Those who want to pursue integrity must embody it in every action, decision, and interaction. Those who choose integrity choose long-term strength and credibility.

As you navigate your journey, it is vital to reflect on your choices as you make them. This will make it easier to resist rationalization and continuously commit to integrity.

Integrity reigns above all traits. Integrity is the true measure of greatness.

Your choices define your legacy—will you choose integrity or succumb to rationalization's fleeting but destructive allure?

CHAPTER 5:
PERFECTION IS THE ENEMY OF PROGRESS

"Have no fear of perfection—you'll never reach it."
— Salvador Dalí

The Myth of Flawlessness

Striving for perfection is tempting and, most of the time, commendable. However, the pursuit of such flawlessness can be a trap. When perfection is our ultimate goal, progress can often come to a standstill. Both individuals and organizations have been known to waste time overanalyzing, delaying action, and setting unrealistic standards. Perfectionism creates an illusion of control, but in reality, it prevents growth and stifles innovation.

Why Perfectionism Stalls Action: Real-World Case Studies

Perfection is generally viewed as a positive concept. But seeking it out can be a massive barrier to real progress and growth. When people push relentlessly for flawlessness and perfection, they often end up in a state of paralysis. This paralysis is caused by their intense analysis of every error, potential error, and imperfection. As they focus so intently on pursuing absolute perfection, they begin to scrutinize every action, which simply slows productivity overly.

Realistically, no individual can be perfect. It's simply impossible. So, rather than wasting our time and risking paralysis by pursuing such things, we should strive to embrace excellence instead. Excellence is achievable, more straightforward, and less likely to keep us trapped.

Case Studies in Perfectionism Leading to Failure

Case Study #13 - Kodak: The Photography Giant That Hesitated

Not too long ago, Kodak was more than a mere company. The name was a cultural icon. It was synonymous with capturing memories. After being founded by George Eastman in 1888, Kodak completely revolutionized the world of photography. The brand made photography accessible to millions who cherished having their life's moments printed on Kodak film. By the 1960s and 1970s, Kodak was a globally dominating brand. 85% of camera sales internationally were Kodak purchases, even higher in the United States. Kodak was huge. It wasn't just a camera brand; it had become the brand.

But this dominance and sense of surety planted impossible seeds to unearth. So used to being on top, Kodak became complacent. In 1975, a Kodak engineer named Steve Sasson developed the world's first-ever digital camera. It was an incredible, ground-breaking invention, and yet, when Sasson demonstrated the prototype, Kodak's executives did not see his vision. They saw a threat. Their perfectionism and subsequent purist approach to film photography created a fear of disruption, which closed their eyes to the new invention's extraordinary potential.

The executives rationalized their hesitation, arguing that digital technology was inferior. They called digital tech a "niche fad" that would pass and could never rival film's high quality. In reality, they were concerned that digital cameras would destroy their sales figures and that film photography would suffer due to digital. Once they finally accepted that digital photography was coming onto the market, whether they liked it or not, Kodak endlessly refined their digital prototypes without ever committing fully to a production line. The result? Despite having signed patents, rivals quickly embraced the digital revolution. Companies like Sony, Canon, and even Apple rapidly seized as much market share as possible.

Meanwhile, Kodak watched from the sidelines, immobilized by their perfectionism. They refused to risk imperfection and were immobilized, watching as they slowly lost relevance in a rapidly digitizing world. By the new millennium, their market share had plummeted, and they were all but obsolete.

Eventually, Kodak belatedly entered the digital market in what was clearly a final desperate attempt—but it was far too late. Consumers had moved on, and the competitors in the market had innovated way beyond their initial offerings. Kodak's once-legendary band, synonymous with photography and capturing memories, instead became associated with falling behind and missing opportunities. The company never recovered. In 2012, Kodak filed for bankruptcy.

The story of Kodak underscores the danger of perfectionism when it comes to business decisions. Leaders obsessed with maintaining existing success at the expense of innovation for fear of ruining their perfect brand name or appearance will always find that the stagnation will cost them dearly. Had Kodak's executives prioritized innovation, even at the risk of disrupting their profitable film business, they might have remained photography industry leaders. But now, Kodak brings a cautionary tale: perfectionism will stall progress and prove catastrophic, especially in sectors defined by rapid change.

Case Study #14 – The Concorde: A Technological Marvel That Never Reached Its Potential

British and French engineers developed the Concorde in the 1960s and 1970s, and it was immediately hailed as an extraordinary achievement in aviation technology. It was sleek, with a futuristic aesthetic, and its supersonic capabilities allowed it to travel at twice the speed of sound, which cut transatlantic flight times by more than half. The Concorde symbolized progress, luxury, ingenuity, and style for many people. It was essential to hundreds; even the general public knew the plane's capabilities.

Behind what was a technological marvel, though, was a deep-rooted commitment to perfection that would come to limit The Concorde's potential. Engineers and governments became so overwhelmingly focused on achieving an impeccable and flawless design that practicality and, more importantly, cost were cast aside. They became secondary considerations as every plane component was meticulously crafted to exact standards. Many of these extreme standards surpassed the necessary numbers and limits for safe and effective flight. The work that was done on the Concorde caused all sorts of costs, delays, and even operational inefficiencies.

Concorde's development took significantly longer than anticipated, and its budget quickly ballooned. When it entered commercial service in 1976, the supersonic jet was quickly one of the most expensive aircraft ever built. The perfectionism that went into engineering Concorde created extraordinary maintenance requirements, driving costs even further to unsustainable figures. Ticket prices soared, restricting availability to an exclusive group of wealthy passengers.

Some airlines embraced this level of prestige, but it wasn't long before the economics made it unviable. The aircraft's limited passenger capacity also strained business profitability, and airlines soon struggled to justify the exorbitant ticket prices needed to break even. Despite its appeal and technological brilliance, the perfection-driven costs associated with Concorde dramatically reduced widespread adoption.

The challenges Concorde faced weren't just financial-related, though. There were issues with the aircraft's noise levels and a constant battle over strict noise regulations. There were also gradually increasing concerns about its environmental impact—if a standard aircraft used a reasonable amount of jet fuel, how much was being used for each flight across the Atlantic in Concorde? Not only that, but the perfectionism that had gone into Concorde's design made any adaptations impractical and unaffordable, limiting the aircraft's ability to evolve as the market demands evolved. The most significant and final blow, however, came in 2000, when an Air France Concorde tragically crashed shortly after takeoff. This horrific incident showed that even in a "perfect" craft, there were vulnerabilities and demonstrated that it was perhaps not worth the cost. It also damaged public trust in the craft, harming its popularity.

In 2003, after only 27 years of flying, the Concorde was retired, marking a decidedly disappointing end to an era of innovation and ambition. Concorde now serves as a mere memory and a poignant reminder that perfectionism can severely limit progress and practicality.

If Concorde's creators prioritized cost-efficiency and practicality over perfection, then supersonic travel might've become mainstream rather than an elite luxury. A more balanced approach to the engineering feat could have resulted in an aircraft that traveled at a groundbreaking speed while remaining sustainable, accessible, and cost-effective to both the traveler and those running the airlines.

Concorde's legacy is a critical lesson for innovators and developers that warns of the dangers of pursuing perfection. It tells us clearly that pursuing perfection can and will prevent genuine progress. Instead, we should embrace practical excellence, learn from imperfections, and maintain the flexibility to adapt.

Case Study #15 – The Space Shuttle Challenger Disaster: The Cost of Perfectionism and Complacency

On January 28th, 1986, NASA's Space Shuttle Challenger was ready and waiting to go. Challenger was set to be a mission that would inspire and educate the USA and the world. With a crew of seven, including an American teacher, Christa McAuliffe, the goal was ultimately to bring space exploration into classrooms across the globe.

Challenger's launch was highly anticipated; for many, it represented human achievement and technological excellence, and for thousands across the United States, it symbolized a moment of national pride. Unfortunately, just 73 seconds after liftoff, the Challenger craft tragically disintegrated, and the lives of all on board were tragically lost.

Initial assumptions were that the Challenger disaster was a technological failure. However, it was significantly more profound than that. The Challenger craft's explosion was caused by organizational perfectionism. As an organization, NASA had carefully curated a public image of flawlessness, precision, operational perfection, and engineering excellence. As a result, they fostered a culture resistant to acknowledging, accepting, or addressing imperfections.

Months before the day of the launch, engineers at NASA and Morton Thiokol, the company responsible for producing and engineering the shuttle's solid rocket boosters, expressed grave concerns. They voiced uncertainty about the integrity of critical rubber O-ring seals. The seals were responsible for preventing hot combustion gases from leaking during launch. Engineers discovered during the testing of these O-rings that they were vulnerable at unusually low temperatures, where they become stiff and brittle, losing their ability to maintain a tight seal as needed. NASA, however, dismissed these concerns. Driven by the pressure to adhere to tight launch schedules and maintain a perfect public image, they completely rejected the engineers' voices.

The night before the Challenger launch, Morton Thiokol engineers held an emergency teleconference with NASA. The engineers strongly urged NASA to delay the launch due to forecasted low temperatures. Under the immense pressure to uphold their reputation, though, NASA rationalized the risk. They were unwilling to accept potential imperfections in an otherwise meticulously planned timeline.

As predicted, the morning of the launch was unusually cold. The conditions almost perfectly fit those identified by the engineers as hazardous to the shuttle's all-important O-ring seals. Regardless of these conditions and perils, the countdown proceeded as scheduled, and tragically, as expected, an O-ring failed. Hot gases were allowed to escape, and a catastrophic explosion occurred, shattering NASA's image that they had worked so hard to maintain.

Following the tragedy, an investigation exposed how NASA's institutional perfectionism and bureaucratic complacency had created a dangerous organizational structure and culture. By focusing on projecting perfection, NASA leaders had stifled all critical feedback and actively suppressed dissenting opinions. Engineers were afraid to speak up, fearful that their concerns would be perceived as obstacles rather than safety insights.

The disaster led to the complete rebuilding of the organization. Deep introspection and reforms were done to foster transparency, communication, and humility. The tragedy served as a powerful, sobering reminder that genuine excellence requires addressing imperfections and continuous learning and growth.

The tragedy of that fateful morning could have been prevented if the NASA executives had embraced and encouraged open communication and listened to their collaborators. Instead, the Challenger story became a horrifying cautionary tale and a tragic testament to the consequences of perfectionism.

How to Prioritize Progress Over Perfection

To truly be able to prioritize progress over perfection, you must make a conscious shift in your mindset and, subsequently, in your actions. You must do all that you can to ensure you're encouraging momentum rather than stagnation.

The first step in this process is to embrace development, no matter its form. We must recognize that meaningful advancements often occur incrementally, built on improvement after improvement rather than flawless initial attempts. The greatest innovations in this world are born from the courage to continue in the face of imperfection—the most beautiful works of art, novels, and tech will all have started as, or have been at one stage, flawed. Acknowledging this helps defeat perfectionism, helps us to combat the delays that it causes, and frees our creativity. Imperfection is a natural step toward improvement, and we must embrace it in order to develop a culture of experimentation and innovation!

Organizational cultures that punish mistakes or that overly criticize imperfections are inherently discouraging innovation. The trick to success is to reward experimentation—successful businesses like Google, for example, have projects like the "moonshot factory" which encourage ambition, even if it initially involves trial and error. Leaders must focus on recognizing when work is developed enough to move forward, and on allowing individuals to continuously develop products and projects in order to achieve the best results. Focusing on perfection is pointless, as not only will it lead to stagnation and complacency, but it is inherently subjective, and therefore can never truly be reached.

When we prioritize completion over perfection, we can safely ensure that projects reach their intended audience and actually get the chance to generate real-world impact. If we embrace iteration, the practice of making continual improvements post-launch, we can foster growth and learning. Embracing this allows us to reframe mistakes as valuable learning experiences rather than setbacks, which is a frame of mind that can be beneficial in encouraging resilience and ongoing development.

Taking action even when faced with uncertainty is crucial, since so many groundbreaking and world-changing achievements and innovations begin in conditions of imperfection. Those who seek to innovate should start immediately, rather than waiting for the "perfect" conditions, and when they've got a functioning or complete project, should allow it to enter the world, refining it as they go. External perspectives from mentors, peers and users will only help to better your ideas, improve your project and find faults that you may have perhaps not noticed.

Ultimately, understanding that continuous improvement yields better results than an unrealistic and unattainable pursuit of perfection frees people and organizations to achieve greater heights.

Key Takeaways

- Prioritize iterative development and continuous improvement over flawless initial outcomes.
- Create organizational cultures that embrace experimentation and calculated risks.
- Promote transparency and open dialogue about imperfections and challenges.
- Set realistic, flexible goals to encourage steady progress.

Final Thoughts

It may feel like perfection is what we should all reach for, but time and time again, history has repeatedly provided examples that demonstrate how perfectionism hinders more than it helps.

Consider Kodak's hesitation to embrace new industry standards in the form of digital photography, and the Concorde's constant quest for true perfection, as well as NASA's tragic Challenger disaster—each of these serves as a powerful reminder that pursuing perfection frequently prevents sustainable innovation and advancement.

What history shows us is that true progress actually starts with the courage to act in the face of uncertainty and imperfection. True success and progress rely on our ability to accept and learn from our mistakes rather than fear them. When we are equipped with the wisdom to value continuous improvement, we can begin to move forward, refining our approaches through experience and feedback instead of stagnating under unrealistic standards that we have set ourselves.

Innovators throughout history who have left their footprint on society understood this principle. Thomas Edison, famous for his invention of the electric lightbulb, remarked after several attempts, "I have not failed. I've just found 10,000 ways that won't work." His perspective is further evidence that genuine breakthroughs require embracing imperfections and failures as necessary steps towards success.

Similarly, pioneering organizations like Amazon and Netflix have thrived by prioritizing innovation, experimentation, and rapid iteration over flawless execution. Amazon founder Jeff Bezos emphasizes a "Day 1" mindset—encouraging continuous innovation, embracing failure as a learning opportunity, and maintaining momentum rather than seeking perfection. Netflix consistently tests new features, learning quickly from feedback, adjusting strategies, and rapidly evolving to meet market demands.

Perfectionism, conversely, often leads to frustration, missed opportunities, and stagnation. Recognizing the difference between healthy ambition and detrimental perfectionism is essential for sustained progress. Excellence encourages consistent effort, resilience, and adaptability; perfectionism induces fear, anxiety, and paralysis.

Ultimately, progress depends not on the absence of mistakes but on the ability to learn, adapt, and improve continuously. Organizations and leaders that prioritize progress over perfection foster environments where innovation thrives, collaboration strengthens, and meaningful accomplishments emerge.

As you reflect on your journey, remember that your legacy will be defined not by flawless execution but by the willingness to pursue progress courageously despite uncertainty. Imperfections are inevitable, but they are also valuable teachers.

Embrace them with humility, curiosity, and resilience, and you will discover imperfection itself often guides the most significant advancements and be the pathway to true progress.

Choose progress over perfection, growth over stagnation, and action over hesitation. Doing so unleashes your true potential and creates lasting impact and innovation. Progress, not perfection, is the true hallmark of meaningful achievement.

CHAPTER 6
TRADITION IS THE ENEMY OF INNOVATION

"Tradition is not the worship of ashes, but the preservation of fire." — Gustav Mahler

The Double-Edged Sword of Tradition

Tradition is important. For many, it is the source of continuity, memory, identity, and stability. Traditions can act as a societal glue, fostering unity and a collective sense of purpose. They offer frameworks and guidelines that help people navigate the present and their community by drawing on age-old lessons from the past.

When the desire to adhere to tradition becomes too strong, it can stifle innovation, growth, and progress. Societies, organizations, and people too often cling to established norms, resisting what is necessary change when new approaches promise significant, exciting change or benefits. This hesitation and fear of disrupting the familiar has been known to sow scientific breakthroughs in the past. It has delayed vital social reforms and caused previously powerful institutions to decline. Tradition is where much of the skepticism that innovation faces when it emerges comes from. Where innovation pushes boundaries and often questions or sometimes even draws attention to long-term instilled beliefs and practices, it disrupts those long-standing traditions.

This tension between tradition and progress remains pervasive today, influencing industries, institutions, and personal decisions across the globe.

When Stagnation Masquerades as Stability

Plenty of people are attached to tradition for various reasons—they may feel it promises stability, for example. What they often don't consider, though, is that stability can quickly become stagnation. Organizations and societies all too often mistake conformity to these traditions for strength and stability, but they fail to recognize when that stability is masking resistance to beneficial changes. The comfort that they take from the familiarity of tradition becomes an illusion of security and safety; all the while, beneath the surface, their stagnation erodes their creativity.

These stagnant organizations and communities frequently suffer from reduced adaptability alongside outdated methodologies. Nokia, for example, fell from its role as a leader in the industry for that very reason. Having once been synonymous with mobile phones, Nokia refused to budge from its traditional model, ignoring the growing demand for smartphones and general innovation. Instead, the company remained committed to traditional and pre-established practices, which blinded the company to the revolutionary untapped potential of touchscreen technology. Ultimately, this led to the company's collapse as competitors like Apple and Samsung jumped in and seized the opportunity.

Had Nokia maintained the competitive edge they had been known for before the emergence of smartphones, they could have embraced innovation and jumped at the opportunity to revolutionize their organization. Instead, the company lost out and very quickly began to decline.

Case Study #16: The Church vs. Galileo: Suppression of Science

In the 17th century, Galileo, an Italian mathematician and astronomer, turned his telescope to the sky and, unexpectedly, caught something incredible. He spotted Jupiter's moons, phases of Venus, and lunar craters. All of this counted as evidence that directly challenged centuries of beliefs that placed the Earth at the center of the universe—evidence evolving from the teachings of Aristotle and Ptolemy and supported by the Catholic church.

Galileo initially thought his discoveries would be welcomed and celebrated. The reality, however, was very different. Instead, they were met with hostility, skepticism, and actual condemnation from the religious authorities. Church leaders saw Galileo's findings as a direct assault on the biblical approach and interpretations and a threat to the ecclesiastical authority. Tradition was the key to the church's power, and challenging that tradition and its established beliefs was considered dangerous heresy.

Despite the mounting hostility, Galileo published his findings and passionately defended them. In 1633, he was summoned before the Roman Inquisition under charges of heresy. Under threat of torture and death, he forcibly abandoned his discoveries, publicly disavowing all that he'd learned. As a result, he was spared a painful death, but he spent his remaining years locked up under house arrest, humiliated and silenced.

The Church's rigidity around its tradition had severe consequences. It suppressed scientific advancement and, as a result, dramatically stalled intellectual progress. Galileo's work was banned and censored, but it spread underground at a much slower rate than it would have had it been freely available. Scientists became wary, fearful of suffering prosecution for their findings, which led the pace of discovery and scientific progress in Europe to slow dramatically.

Truth prevailed; centuries later, the church acknowledged Galileo's discoveries as scientifically accurate and officially admitted error in silencing him. Pope John Paul II formally recognized his contributions in 1992—over three centuries later. The Pope acknowledged that dogmatic rigidity had severely hindered progress, something that had been clear for some time.

In a world where the church had embraced Galileo's findings and fostered dialogue rather than imposing silence, perhaps the Renaissance might have come around even faster. Maybe more advancements could've been ignited, and we'd have seen an even bigger boom across astronomy, physics, and mathematics decades earlier. Instead, the traditions that the church saw as a stabilizing force became a barrier, preventing society from embracing critical scientific truths.

Galileo's struggle embodies the timeless tension between tradition and innovation. The tragedy of his story emphasizes how important it is that tradition should never justify silencing the truth. Galileo understood this and believed tradition should serve truth, not suppress it. Famously, he argued, "I do not feel obliged to believe that the same God who endowed us with sense, reason, and intellect has intended us to forgo their use."

Galileo's persecution offers crucial lessons about the dangers of placing tradition above curiosity. It shows us that actual progress emerges from the courage to challenge, question, and, importantly, remain open to uncomfortable truths, even if those truths shake our beliefs to their core. When religious, social, or political institutions stick to tradition instead of welcoming innovation and exploration, they risk becoming oppressive rather than enlightening.

Today, this story stands as a symbol of intellectual freedom's eventual triumph over dogmatic tradition. Galileo's legacy should inspire people to challenge conventional wisdom boldly and remind us that tradition can offer wisdom but should never become an unchallengeable barrier.

Case Study #17 – The Wright Brothers: Defying Conventional Wisdom

At the turn of the 20th century, it was generally accepted that human flight was impossible. It was a fantastical notion that had been relegated to myth and fiction. Esteemed scientists, intellectuals, and even prominent academics ridiculed the idea that humans could ever build a machine that would be capable of sustained, powered flight. In fact, scientific institutions went as far as confidently lamenting that such pursuits were foolish and defied the "fundamental laws of nature."

Two humble bicycle mechanics from Dayton, Ohio, weren't having any of it. Wilbur and Orville Wright saw the world differently from others. The pair were driven by boundless curiosity and unwavering belief that human flight was achievable. The Wright brothers dared to question the generally accepted truth. Other peoples' skepticism didn't deter them, nor did the dismissive attitudes of academics. The brothers had an experimental mindset and started working on their ideas. They meticulously tested hypotheses, learning from every setback. Each time they failed, they took notes and returned to work.

Working in their bicycle shop, they conducted experiments with homemade gliders and aerodynamic models. They analyzed the lift, thrust, and control factors and documented their tests. Each test allowed them to refine their calculations and question established theories. They incrementally improved their models, advancing their understanding of aerodynamics and mechanics as they went.

On December 17th, 1903, their work took them to the sands of Kitty Hawk, North Carolina, where the Wright Flyer took off despite every scientific voice telling them it was impossible. It was a groundbreaking moment in history, marking the very first controlled, sustained, powered flight ever in human history. By working together in their bike store, they'd achieved what everyone had said was impossible. They'd put humans in the air, proving the prevailing scientific opinion wrong.

However, the Wright brothers faced doubt and dismissal from the scientific and engineering communities even after their breakthrough. Everyone, scientists, journalists, and even military leaders, brushed off their accomplishment, claiming that they must exaggerate or fabricate their results. The Wright brothers persisted, though, and continued to demonstrate their aircraft publicly while working behind the scenes and improving its performance and safety as they tried to silence skeptics.

Eventually, the undeniable results compelled the scientific world to recognize the reality: human flight was possible, and the Wright brothers fundamentally transformed transportation. Their success laid the foundation for aviation engineering and science, taking humanity into a new era of global connection.

Progress could have accelerated faster if the scientific community embraced the Wright brothers from the outset. More open-minded support and collaborative work could have spurred rapid advancements, potentially hastening innovations such as passenger air travel or aerospace technology.

The story of the Wright Brothers is another example that demonstrates the importance of challenging tradition and assumption, welcoming new perspectives, and embracing innovation, even in the face of skepticism and resistance. The Wright Brothers' courage to continue to defy conventional opinion transformed human history, highlighting how genuine progress often requires the courage to push boundaries and question tradition.

Case Study #18: The Bitcoin Revolution: Shaking Traditional Finance

In 2009, when Bitcoin first emerged, the world was in the midst of a global financial crisis. Bitcoin was created by an essentially complete mystery, a figure known as Satoshi Nakamoto, and it offered a new approach to the world of finance. What Bitcoin offered was free of the control of banks, governments, and financial intermediaries. Its decentralized blockchain technology promised complete transparency, autonomy, and security, challenging the long-held traditions of centralized monetary tech and systems.

To begin with, traditional banks and bodies dismissed Bitcoin as nothing more than a speculative curiosity. They labeled it as impractical at best and a potential threat at worst. Financial institutions were convinced that a decentralized currency was unrealistic and outright unsustainable. Authorities simply seemed concerned about the lack of control, concerned that Bitcoin would be used as a tool for criminal activity.

While the mainstream institutions hesitated, innovative fintech startups and daring entrepreneurs jumped aboard. They quickly recognized the potential and understood the utterly transformative power of blockchain technology, decentralized finance platforms, and exchanges that, at their core, gave ordinary people unprecedented access and control over their financial resources. Within a decade, cryptocurrencies rapidly evolved from fringe experiments into mainstream financial opportunities. They had caught global attention and were attracting trillions of dollars worth of market value.

By the time traditional financial institutions recognized their error in dismissing Bitcoin, they were playing catch up. They had denied the innovation, which quickly matured into a significant financial market. This forced banks to invest heavily to remain relevant. In the meantime, fintech organizations like Coinbase, Binance, and Kraken had secured substantial market shares and redefined financial transactions worldwide.

This sudden shift toward decentralized finance revealed a vulnerability in the traditional banking systems. Traditional banks had grown complacent in their longstanding and presumed eternal dominance. Major banks had been forced to scramble to develop blockchain-based systems and to adopt digital currencies, and even then, their initial resistance had cost them dearly.

Had the traditional institutions recognized Bitcoin's potential and adopted blockchain tech sooner, they could have positioned themselves as leaders or innovators. Instead, their need to uphold tradition and skepticism toward new and disruptive tech limited their adaptability. This resulted in lost opportunities and diminished influence.

The Bitcoin revolution is a great example of the profound cost that tradition can have. It once again shows us that true innovation demands openness to change and adaptability.

Balancing Heritage with Innovation

Tradition can indeed hinder us, but it's also true that tradition is incredibly important to plenty of people and cultures. As a result, we must work to balance tradition and innovation in a way that allows us to respect and preserve historical wisdom and tradition while also striving to create an environment conducive to conceiving fresh ideas.

Companies like LEGO understand this approach. When faced with threats from digital video games, LEGO innovated within its traditional domain. They developed digital strategies and partnerships, allowing them to take the necessary step forward into a new market while still appreciating and valuing the traditional values that had helped them get there.

Key Takeaway

Freeing ourselves from tradition's grip requires proactivity and bravery. We must question assumptions and traditions held sacred or truthfully by those who came before us but no longer serve a meaningful purpose. To prevent stagnation, we, as people and even organizations, must have the courage to confront outdated practices, challenge them, and be open to new possibilities.

We must welcome experimentation, even when we value tradition. To free ourselves from the grips of our traditions, we need to be ready to innovate and to learn from failure. To do this, we must encourage an open dialogue within our communities and organizations. This will help to foster the innovative mindset necessary for progress.

It may be essential to prevent tradition from causing us to stagnate, but it is equally important that we don't just cast tradition aside. To balance tradition and progress, we have to be able to recognize signs of stagnation and take those as a signal that it is time to adapt to the traditions that no longer serve us. We must understand that tradition is a guide, connecting us to our values and heritage, but it should not hold us back. By continuously challenging the comfort of "how things have always been," we pave the way for a dynamic, innovative future.

Final Thoughts

Tradition and innovation are locked in a constant, delicate dance. They continuously shape human progress; tradition provides essential stability, offering us lessons from our history, while innovation drives us forward, challenging established beliefs and prompting evolution. Both elements can coexist despite their seemingly contradictory natures, so long as they are approached carefully.

The critical task for people, societies, and organizations is acknowledging when tradition leads that dance. When tradition overtakes, it stops supporting growth and begins to restrict it. If we adhere unquestioningly to its rules, we too can fall into the trap of rigidity, preventing essential adaptation in our rapidly changing world. Equally importantly, though, we must be able to hold onto our traditions and use them to shape our innovation. Unchecked innovation risks losing valuable historical lessons and cultural continuity.

True success and wisdom lie in striking a delicate balance between tradition and innovation. We must value tradition enough to maintain stability yet be flexible enough to welcome change. This perfect balance creates resilience, adaptability, and truly sustainable growth.

Leadership is vital in navigating this balance. There have been visionary leaders who did not understand how to manage it. The ideal leadership encourages experimentation, values new ideas, and always remains open to transformative ideas.

By following that lead and honoring the past while simultaneously daring to explore what the future holds, we unlock potential. With this, we can create organizations and societies that are vibrant and continuously evolving. With tradition and innovation working together, we can harness their power and continue to grow.

The question is: Are you holding on to tradition at the expense of progress, or are you willing to innovate for a better tomorrow?"

CHAPTER 7:
LOYALTY IS THE ENEMY OF FREEDOM

"Blind loyalty is an empty gesture that shackles us to the past and prevents us from stepping into the future." — Unknown.

The Double-Edged Sword of Loyalty

Loyalty is often regarded as a virtue, as a symbol of honor, trust, and commitment. While it can be all those things, loyalty is a double-edged sword. It can also be insidious, sinister, and corruptive. Loyalty creates bonds that can be deeply meaningful and enduring, but when taken to extremes, it can blind individuals to the truth. It can force them to betray their values and strip them of their ability to think and act freely.

It can become a powerful weapon of control when loyalty goes unchecked. It is what keeps people devoted to corrupt leaders and oppressive institutions out of obligation. Their refusal to challenge authority, even when seemingly necessary, has led to personal ruin for many, as well as political disasters and even organizational collapses.

Loyalty can be important, but true freedom comes when we avoid blind allegiance and keep the courage to question, reassess, and, when necessary, to walk away.

When Stagnation Masquerades as Stability – Real-World Case Studies

Loyalty can easily create an illusion of stability if placed above our critical thought. This stability has been the root of people and institutions clinging to established relationships, leaders, and systems. The stability they feel leads them to believe that breaking away would send them into chaos. But in reality, history has shown us that this sort of unchallenged loyalty often results in stagnation, corruption, and eventual collapse.

One such example is the Roman Republic; citizens loyal to Rome's traditional politics remained fiercely loyal even as the political structures became noticeably unfit for governing. Instead of adapting, Rome's elite resisted reform. The result was increasing power struggles and, eventually, the collapse of the Republic.

Case Study #19 – The Fall of the Roman Republic: When Loyalty Destroys Democracy

The Roman Republic began in 509 BCE when the Romans overthrew their monarchy and decided to try something new. It was founded on the principles of shared governance, representative leadership, and strict systems to keep anyone from gaining too much control. The setup worked remarkably well, especially for a city-state trying to hold things together through collective rule. Over time, it helped Rome to flourish as one of the most powerful empires in history, spreading its influence as it conquered vast territories and influenced civilizations far beyond the Italian peninsula. Ironically, though, it was that very success that planted the seeds of the Republic's eventual downfall. The deep sense of loyalty that had once held Rome together became rigid and destructive.

Romans took immense pride in their institutions, traditions, and laws in the Republic's prime. Senators and citizens with a stake in the system were particularly invested and loyal to the new system. However, as Rome expanded its borders, the existing political system struggled to keep up. It was not designed to manage a sprawling empire encompassing diverse people, distant territories, and complicated issues. Despite this, the Roman elite clung tightly to the old ways out of fear of undermining their privileged positions. Any attempt to reform the system was dismissed as dangerous and even sacrilegious until it was clear that protecting tradition mattered more than solving the problem.

By the first century BCE, cracks in the Republic had become impossible to ignore. Corruption, inequality, and power struggles were endemic. The Senate, meant to guide the state, often acted to protect its own interests instead. Reformers endeavored to fix things, offering populist solutions to problems like land reform or citizenship for Rome's non-Italian subjects, but they were suppressed. What had once been loyalty to a noble Republic among the elite became blind devotion to a broken system, all to keep themselves safe and privileged.

Amidst this chaos, Julius Ceaser, a charismatic military commander, stepped onto the stage. A skilled general and a savvy politician, he could see the dysfunction. His popularity grew exponentially, thanks to his military victories and his ability to really connect with "normal" Romans. In 49 BCE, he made a courageous move by crossing the Rubicon River with his army, initiating a civil war that would permanently alter Rome's trajectory. For those still loyal to the Republic, it was a moment of treason. Still, for those who had lost their allegiance, it was a necessary rebellion against a government that was no longer serving their citizens.

Caesar won the war and received unprecedented powers, which made him a dictator for life. In 44 BCE, senators who had been intensely loyal to the old order, including Brutus and Cassius, assassinated Caesar, hoping it would restore the system they had cherished. In reality, it just triggered even more instability and violence. Their loyalty had closed their eyes to the reality that Rome had already changed.

In the aftermath, Caesar's adopted heir, Octavian (later Augustus), seized control. He became Rome's first emperor in 27 BCE, carefully preserving the appearance of the republic and hiding his autocratic rule behind it. Soldiers no longer pledged their allegiance to Rome or its laws but to Augustus. The shift was initially subtle for many, but it was soon evident. Loyalty had become personal, not institutional. This only embedded dangerous instability at the foundation of the Ronan Empire, as future emperors would exploit military loyalty for personal gain.

As the empire progressed, this new unchecked loyalty fueled cycles of violence and instability. Emperors came and went, often through force or assassination, and backed by armies whose loyalty was conditional and opportunistic. Laws or shared values no longer guided the system but by power plays and personal alliances. By the third century BCE, Rome had become dangerously fragmented. It had been weakened from within by power struggles and unended internal conflicts. When external enemies pressed in, the empire had no choice but to succumb. There was no strength or unity to stand firm, and collapse was inevitable.

Rome's tragic story is a powerful warning about what happens when loyalty is misplaced. If Rome's senators had embraced change instead of clinging to their tradition-bound past, the outcome could have been very different if soldiers had stayed loyal to the Republic instead of to individual men. Instead, they lost the very thing they were trying to protect by holding on too tightly to outdated structures.

The fall of the Roman Republic offers us an important lesson: loyalty isn't always a virtue. Unquestioning loyalty to updated structures can suffocate people and organizations, erode strength, and trigger the collapse of relationships, societies, and organizations. To be helpful, loyalty must be paired with flexibility, critical reflection, and a willingness to evolve.

Case Study #20 – The Jonestown Massacre: Loyalty's Dangerous Consequence

In November 1978, the world watched in shock and horror as unexpected, horrifying news emerged from a remote jungle in Guyana. Over 900 people were dead. Men, women, and children had all lost their lives in what became one of the most extensive mass deaths of the 20th century. All 900 of the lives lost were tied to one man, a manipulator who twisted their loyalty into a nightmare: Reverend Jim Jones. He founded the community in Guyana known as Jonestown and led his ministry there.

At first, it felt impossible. The story was so surreal. People at home struggled to grasp how so many seemingly intelligent people ended up in such a dark place. It simply wouldn't compute—because the answer wasn't simple. This wasn't a sudden event but the culmination of years of slow, calculated manipulation. Trust, loyalty, and hope had been twisted beyond recognition into tools of control.

Jim Jones began his ministry in the 1950s, presenting himself as a passionate advocate for racial equality. He was charismatic, compelling and preached equality, racial integration, and social justice. His message initially attracted thousands of followers from all sorts of diverse backgrounds, many of whom were educated, socially conscious, and deeply committed to building a better world. Jones offered them what appeared to be a real, progressive alternative to mainstream society, where racial integration, social justice, and community solidarity would be held as core values.

As Jones' popularity grew, he established the Peoples Temple. Initially, the temple was viewed as an inclusive haven for racial harmony, social activism, and community service. It fought for the marginalized, offered food and support to the poor, and upheld this image of a loving, progressive community. The organization gained powerful political allies, and Jones even received recognition for his humanitarian work. However, beneath Jones' idealistic rhetoric lay something more sinister: a ruthless desire for absolute power and unquestioned loyalty.

Over time, Jones shifted, and where loyalty to him and the temple had once been a choice for those within the Temple, it quickly became a requirement, an unquestionable command. Questioning him was framed as betrayal, and doubt was dangerous. Members of the Peoples Temple were systematically indoctrinated to equate devotion with unquestioning obedience. Those who dared to speak out were shamed, isolated, or punished. Bit by bit, the followers gave up pieces of their freedom in the name of the unity they had joined seeking.

Even then, despite Jones' growing paranoia, drug use, and cruel punishments inflicted on dissenting members, most of Jones' followers remained fiercely loyal. The idea of betraying their leader, who had successfully convinced them he was their protector, became inconceivable.

To solidify his control, Jones isolated followers from external influences. In the 1970s, when the media started looking into the Temple's darker side following accusations of abuse, coercion, and manipulation, Jones fled the spotlight. He led his followers to Guyana, miles away from the media's scrutiny, and where he could build Jonestown. He called it a paradise, a utopia free from the corruption of the outside world, but in reality, it was a prison in the jungle. Cut off, isolated, and under Jones' total control, members were subjected to relentless propaganda and fear.

In November 1978, the situation escalated. Concerned about possible abuse following relatives' reports, U.S. Congressman Leo Ryan traveled to Jonestown to see things for himself. He and his team were initially welcomed. However, they could sense that there was more at play below the surface. When they tried to leave with a handful of defectors, gunmen from the Temple ambushed them near the airstrip and killed Leo Ryan and four other people.

Jim Jones knew what came next. He understood that authorities would soon arrive. So he told his followers that the end was near, that they were under attack, and that they had no way out. In his final speech, he painted mass suicide as a revolutionary act. He framed it as a protest, a moment of dignity. Many of his followers believed him, and those who didn't were made to come around to the idea through persuasion, fear, or force. In the end, over 900 people drank cyanide-laced Flavor-Aid. More than 300 of the bodies found after the fact were children. 900 people lost their lives, not only to the poison but to their unquestioning loyalty and indoctrination that eroded their ability to question, to doubt—to say no.

The Jonestown horror forced the world to confront the deeply uncomfortable truth: loyalty can be dangerous when it replaces independent thought. The people who died at Jonestown were educated, thoughtful individuals. They were idealists, dreamers, parents, and activists, and they all died because their loyalty had replaced their autonomy.

What happened in Jonestown could have been prevented if critical thinking and dissent had been fostered rather than crushed. Former members and journalists alike had raised alarms, but their cries were dismissed, minimized, and ignored. The Temple's good public image made it all too easy to look the other way simply.

The tragedy that took place leaves us with a powerful and painful lesson: loyalty must be monitored. It must never come at the expense of truth, reason, or conscience. True loyalty is not silent; it asks questions, allows disagreement, and, most importantly, respects the right to walk away.

Case Study #21 – Bernie Madoff: Loyalty Blinding Investors to Fraud

As the 20th century ended, Bernie Madoff was a towering figure on Wall Street, who enjoyed near-unparalleled respect and trust in financial circles—essentially, he was revered. To many, he was the very picture of Wall Street success. As the founder of Bernard L. Madoff Investment Securities LLC, he earned himself a reputation for delivering steady, impressive returns even during economic crises.

His clients, ranging from banks to charities to individuals, trusted him implicitly with their financial futures. Many even considered themselves lucky to have access to him. His clients were nothing short of believers in a man who seemed to be able to defy the odds and deliver results when others couldn't.

However, something much darker was behind the polished exterior and calm assurance. Madoff's empire wasn't built on genius. It was built on lies. He had been orchestrating a massive Ponzi scheme, using money from new investors to pay off older ones, all while maintaining this appearance of success and wealth.

Loyalty, a virtue that once bonded Madoff's customers to him, came shattering down the second the truth was revealed. It immediately became clear that loyalty had been twisted into a powerful weapon of manipulation, enabling fraud on a massive scale and causing people to lose an unprecedented amount of money.

Building Trust: The Roots of Loyalty

Bernie Madoff's journey began in the early 1960s as a legitimate trading enterprise. Over the decades, his charm, charisma, and apparent financial acumen attracted a vast and varied clientele. He very quickly developed a reputation. With his easy charm and obvious mastery of the markets, he was viewed as a man of stature who moved effortlessly in elite social circles and generously to charitable causes.

By the time he served as NASDAQ's chairman, Madoff was more than well-known. He'd become iconic. His success seemed bulletproof, and his integrity unquestionable. Clients didn't just trust him. They believed in him. They handed over life savings, retirement funds, and children's college funds—sometimes, they gave Madoff all they had, based purely on the man's reputation and their loyalty.

That's what makes Madoff's story so haunting.

Loyalty Breeding Complacency

Behind the polished image and reputation, though, Bernie Madoff's operation was slowly unraveling into the largest Ponzi scheme the financial world had ever seen. By the late 1980s, his firm had stopped investing in clients' money. Instead, Madoff began using funds from new investors to pay returns to earlier ones. His firm maintained the illusion of reliability, creating and sending beautifully crafted account statements showing steady, almost uncanny profits. The paperwork looked professional. The numbers were consistent. It was all comforting - too comforting.

The powerful loyalty clients felt for Madoff allowed the scheme to continue for so long. Nobody asked hard questions because they thought they didn't need to. Decades of hard work on Madoff's part, or so it seemed, had earned their trust. Many felt lucky to even work with him.

When doubts began to bubble up, when whispers of fraud or skepticism appeared from outsiders, loyal clients doubled down and fiercely defended him. They brushed off the criticism as jealousy or ignorance. Even seasoned financial firms, hedge funds, and regulators overlooked the red flags and were convinced that someone like Madoff couldn't be lying.

Inside the firm, it was no different. Employees, family members, and associates were wrapped in the same complicated web of personal loyalty. Some suspected something was happening, but saying so meant risking their careers, relationships, and place in a prestigious firm. Speaking up wasn't just hard; it felt like betrayal.

Over time, the culture within Madoff's firm became one where silence was encouraged, even rewarded, and loyalty meant keeping your head down. It became an organization where asking questions wasn't just discouraged. It was dangerous.

The Illusion Crumbles: A Betrayal Revealed

When the 2008 financial crisis hit, it pulled the curtain back on several hidden frauds. But nothing prepared the world for the scale of Bernie Madoff's collapse. As markets plummeted and investors panicked, the fragile structure of Madoff's empire quickly collapsed overnight—the carefully constructed illusion he had maintained for decades cracked. The numbers didn't add up. The money simply wasn't there.

In December 2008, the truth had to come out. In a quiet, devastating moment, Madoff sat his two sons down and told them outright: "It was all just one big lie." The empire he had built, the trust he had earned, the wealth he'd promised—all of it had been a mirage.

His sons, who had stood by him with unwavering loyalty for years, were stunned, but they took the information to the authorities. Within days, Madoff was arrested, and the news had a huge impact.

Clients who believed in him were devastated. They'd invested so much more than money in him and were left with nothing. Entire charities were wiped out, and retirement dreams dissolved overnight. Some have lost not just wealth but also relationships, friendships, and faith in the system.

The numbers were shocking. Bernard Madoff's fraud became the most prominent financial scam in history, totaling nearly $65 billion. The collapse of his company not only left catastrophic financial damage in its wake but psychological scars, too. He'd been a trusted friend, a pillar in people's lives, and it had all been false, fed by their loyalty—people felt utterly betrayed.

The Aftermath: Lessons in Loyalty

The following year, in 2009, Madoff was sentenced to 150 years in federal prison. It was a more symbolic than practical sentence, meant to reflect the sheer scale and cruelty of his crimes and betrayal. It was a powerful gesture, but for the thousands of people whose lives had been shattered by his lies, it felt hollow. The damage had been done and could not be undone. For many of them, said damage would ripple across generations.

People who had spent their entire lives saving and planning for the future suddenly found themselves starting over, some in their seventies and eighties. Prestigious charities crumbled, and universities and foundations lost funding. Schools closed.

Looking back, it's easy to wonder: what if? What if someone had pushed harder, asked more questions, or demanded transparency? Had investors or employees balanced their trust with skepticism and insisted hard enough, Madoff's deception might have been exposed much sooner.

Unfortunately, that's the heartbreaking thing about loyalty. When someone seems successful, generous, and admired, people want to believe in them. They want to feel safe in their loyalty and trust. And in Madoff's case, that allowed his lie to grow until it was too big to ignore.

The Vital Balance

The Bernie Madoff scandal is a powerful reminder of loyalty's complicated nature. At its best, loyalty can unite people, foster trust, and create a sense of belonging and stability. But when it goes unchecked and replaces critical thinking with a sense of blind faith, it can become dangerous.

Bernie Madoff's story isn't just about financial fraud. It's a story of what happens when people stop asking questions. People believed in him, not just his skills but his character. They trusted in him so deeply that they didn't feel the need to ask how their money was being managed. When questions did arise, this loyalty to Madoff kept people silent, and that silence allowed the lie to grow.

The case of Bernie Madoff demonstrates that loyalty without ethics, transparency, and accountability destroys trust. Madoff's victims weren't foolish; they were human. They wanted to believe in a man who offered them success and safety. But had they thought to ask the hard questions or been encouraged to scrutinize, the outcome could have been very different. A few skeptical voices could have stopped a $65 billion fraud case and spared thousands from ruin.

Loyalty should be a force that uplifts and protects, not one that blinds us. When it turns into obedience at the expense of truth, the cost of loyalty can be devastating. Madoff's legacy is a tragic reminder that absolute trust is not built on silence and admiration; it is grounded in openness, courage, and freedom.

Mastering Loyalty: Action Steps for Preserving Freedom

Loyalty is one of the most cherished human values. It allows us to build trust, deepen relationships, and help communities and relationships weather the most brutal storms. But history has shown us time and time again that when loyalty goes unquestioned, it can become dangerous. From the fall of the Roman Republic to the Jonestown tragedy and the financial devastation caused by Bernie Madoff, there are plenty of examples of how loyalty, when not balanced by critical thinking, can lead people down the wrong path.

We must make conscious choices if we want to remain loyal without losing our freedom or integrity. Here's how:

Step 1: *Cultivate Critical Thinking and Encourage Questions*

Unquestioning loyalty tends to grow in places where asking questions and critical thinking feels risky. Whether it's a political regime, a cult, or a corporation, the pattern is the same: they thrive on silence and unquestioned obedience. A culture that values loyalty or wants sustainable and healthy loyalty needs to create space for curiosity and honest dialogue.

One example is Pizar. They've built a creative powerhouse by not shutting down criticism—instead, they invite it in. Ed Catmull, the co-founder, set up a process called "Braintrust." Through these "Braintrust" meetings, employees at all levels give one another feedback. No power dynamics are at play; people are just trying to improve one another. That's what honest loyalty looks like. It's not about nodding along; it's about caring enough to speak up.

Unquestioning loyalty flourishes where critical thinking is discouraged. History repeatedly shows that oppressive regimes, destructive cults, and unethical corporations thrive on followers' silence and unquestioned obedience. A culture that genuinely values loyalty must also value skepticism, curiosity, and questioning.

Step 2: *Establish Transparent Accountability*

Loyalty should never be an excuse to look the other way. Madoff's fraud continued for decades because people trusted his reputation and didn't dig deeper. Accountability structures failed: no one effectively challenged the inconsistencies staring everyone in the face.

If we look at companies like Patagonia, on the other hand, people trust the brand because it's honest. They admit their mistakes and focus on operating transparently and ethically. Their willingness to admit fault publicly shows that they hold themselves to a high standard and have integrity.

Step 3: *Recognize the Difference Between Loyalty and Obedience*

Absolute loyalty doesn't mean following orders without thinking. It means staying true to your values, even if that means pushing back. Healthy loyalty welcomes dissent and questions and even acknowledges that both are necessary for improvement and progress.

The U.S. military is a key example of this. While obedience is a key part of military culture, today's soldiers are taught to refuse any unlawful or unethical commands outright. This came after tragedies like the My Lai Massacre showed what can happen when obedience is valued above conscience. Now, soldiers are expected to think critically, even in the most structured environments.

Step 4: Foster Ethical Courage and Moral Leadership

Blind loyalty doesn't just happen. It's often encouraged by leaders who fear being challenged. The best leaders, though, are those who genuinely prioritize ethics over personal gain, welcome scrutiny, accept feedback, and are not afraid to change course when needed.

Nelson Mandela showed us how powerful this kind of ethical leadership can be. After years in prison, he didn't seek revenge. He stayed loyal to a dream of a just and inclusive South Africa. His loyalty remained grounded in values, not personal power.

Key Takeways

- Loyalty can create meaningful bonds and stability, but when blind and unquestioning, it becomes a dangerous force that stifles freedom and progress.
- Unchecked loyalty traps individuals in oppressive relationships, corrupt institutions, and outdated systems, leading to stagnation, personal ruin, and societal collapse.
- Loyalty must coexist with transparency, critical thinking, accountability, and ethical judgment. Organizations and societies thrive when loyalty is balanced by openness and dissent.
- Individuals and organizations must regularly reassess where they place their loyalty, ensuring it empowers growth and integrity rather than obedience and stagnation.
- True loyalty empowers freedom, adaptation, and growth, while blind loyalty suffocates independence, leading to inevitable ruin.

Final Thoughts

Loyalty is a beautiful thing. It brings people together at its best and gives us something bigger than ourselves to believe in. But when unchecked, loyalty morphs into blind obedience. It undermines personal freedom, clouds our moral compass, and leads us into harm's way.

History has given us plenty of examples of loyalty leading to ruin, whether in the downfall of nations, the rise of dangerous cults, or cases of corporate fraud. From the collapse of the Roman Republic to the heartbreaking example of Jonestown, we see the same pattern: loyalty is dangerous when it stops asking questions.

Take the Roman Republic, for example; its government worked for centuries—until it didn't. As Rome grew into a sprawling empire, the old system struggled to keep up, yet many senators clung to it out of loyalty. They assumed that protecting the past was the same as protecting the future. This unwillingness to adapt created a vacuum, and Julius Ceasar was all too ready to fill it. In trying to remain loyal to something that no longer worked, the Senate helped end the republic.

Then there's Jonestown. An unthinkable tragedy where loyalty turned into blind devotion. Jim Jones demanded total allegiance from his followers, equating doubt with betrayal. Even when it became clear that he was unraveling, most stayed. By the time he ordered a mass suicide, many felt they had no way out. Jonestown reminds us that unchecked loyalty can override personal judgment when used as a weapon against us.

In the case of Bernard Madoff, the danger wasn't dramatic sermons or emotional manipulation. Instead, it was quiet trust. Madoff didn't demand loyalty; he earned it—or so it seemed. Investors remained fiercely loyal to Madoff because of his charm, credibility, and reputation. The financial devastation that followed revealed a painful truth: loyalty becomes a liability without scrutiny or accountability.

One simple truth ties all of these stories together: loyalty becomes dangerous when it silences critical voices and suppresses dissent. History repeatedly demonstrates that true loyalty should never be absolute.

True loyalty that builds something meaningful should never come at the cost of anything. It isn't about saying yes; it's about standing up, speaking out, choosing to stay, and not being forced to. The most significant advancements in human history have come from those who dared to question whether you look at Galileo challenging the geocentric view of the universe or the abolitionists standing against slavery. The most meaningful relationships are built on mutual respect, trust, shared values, and loyalty—not blind allegiance.

To master loyalty, we must create spaces where people are encouraged to speak up, where leaders are held accountable, and where tradition is not more important than progress. We must never expect loyalty to silence questions or discourage debate. It must keep the same value as innovation and curiosity. Only when we reach this balance have we mastered it.

Plenty of great organizations and societies have embraced this balance. The abolitionists who opposed slavery in America were initially condemned as disloyal to tradition, but their courage to question societal norms forged a path to freedom and equality. They broke free from the loyalty they were expected to feel for their society for the sake of their fellow men. Likewise, whistleblowers who risk their jobs to reveal corporate wrongdoing demonstrate profound loyalty—not to flawed leaders, but to ethics and justice!

The takeaway is not that loyalty is terrible; it is far from it. Loyalty can be one of the most potent forces for good when it's aligned with truth, integrity, and justice. Its value depends entirely upon what or whom loyalty serves and the work put into ensuring our loyalty remains aligned with those causes.

In our fast-changing world, fraught with political divides and charismatic leaders seeking unquestioned allegiance, it's more important than ever that we approach loyalty with vigilance and intelligence.

Ask yourself honestly: is my allegiance fostering growth, openness, and integrity? Is my loyalty building something real and lasting? Or is it asking me to ignore my values for the sake of belonging?

The answer will shape more than just your relationship or reputation. It shapes your legacy.

Our loyalty can bind us, uplift us, and help us stand through the storm. But if we're not careful, it can also blind us. So the choice is yours.

Choose wisely. Your integrity, your freedom, and your legacy depend on it.

EPILOGUE

"Facing the Enemy Within"

On a chilly December morning in 1903, two Dayton, Ohio, bike mechanics stood in a windy field at Kitty Hawk, North Carolina, defying not only gravity but centuries of human doubt. The Wright brothers, Orville and Wilbur, faced more than technical issues that morning. They battled the tough adversaries within: skepticism from their peers, ridicule from established experts, and most frighteningly, perhaps, their internal fears and doubts. Yet on that day, in defiance of tradition, skepticism, and perfectionism, their machine lifted beautifully into the air, humanity's first powered flight. They conquered not just the heavens but the inner demons—fears and doubts that paralyze progress.

Throughout this book, we've walked through numerous aspects of our inner enemies—Ego, Passion, Pride, Rationalization, Perfectionism, Tradition, and Loyalty. These powerful forces reside in each of us. They shape decisions, pick paths, and frequently decide fate. Through examples drawn from history, business, science, and personal stories, we've seen how these inner enemies, if not checked, destroy potential, devastate relationships, eat away at integrity, and block meaningful progress.

We witnessed in the Titanic how arrogance, driven by ego, transformed victory into defeat. The story of Napoleon's doomed invasion of Russia illustrated how passion, unbridled by reason, can transform ambition into catastrophe. The bitter feud between Thomas Edison and Nikola Tesla illustrated how pride can destroy friendship and hinder innovative partnerships. And from Bernie Madoff's gigantic fraud, we witnessed how loyalty, devoid of scrutiny and integrity, accomplishes disaster. From Galileo, we learned how conformity to tradition can strangle progress and silence truth.

All of these tragic and transformative tales have something essential in common: the enemy was always from within, never from outside. It wasn't circumstance, competition, or opposition that resulted in failure or collapse. Instead, every failure resulted from internal factors—a direct result of individuals and institutions succumbing to the darker sides of their nature.

And yet, these traits, as we've also seen, are double-edged swords. Within them lies the seed of greatness and the seed of destruction. Ego, firmly kept in balance, gives us self-confidence and fuels innovation. Passion, well-tempered propels visionary leaders and entrepreneurs. Pride, tempered with humility, can spur healthy competition and self-development. Rationalization, acknowledged and bounded, enables us to question and sharpen moral codes. Loyalty, tempered with accountability, unites and builds trust. Tradition, coupled with innovation, roots us in the past while encouraging new ideas. Perfectionism, channeled in a positive direction, can inspire excellence without inhibiting action.

Facing the Mirror

One general lesson comes up repeatedly: our worst enemies are rarely external; they are in the mirror, hidden within our own reflections. Successful leaders and innovators understand that battling these internal enemies is the most critical step toward lasting success. Indeed, the most challenging and rewarding trip we take is inward, facing the ugly truths about ourselves squarely.

Consider the legendary story of Alfred Nobel. In 1888, a French newspaper mistakenly printed Nobel's obituary, branding him a merchant of death due to his invention of dynamite. Horrified at this negative legacy, Nobel took a candid look at his inner world and recognized his responsibility for shaping the world he lived in. He invested his wealth and fame in establishing the Nobel Prizes, permanently transforming his legacy from death to peace, scientific advancement, and human betterment. Nobel's story embodies the book's final message: that each of us can transform our inner enemies into forces for positive change.

The Courage to Look Inward

This courage—to look inward, question assumptions, and confront the internal enemies undermining our potential—is vital to every entrepreneur, leader, and individual who strives for fulfillment and lasting impact. We saw the stark reality of this in the examples of Theranos and Enron. Both companies thrived on illusions, self-deceptions, ego-driven, prideful, and blind loyalty. If only their leaders had the humility and courage to question themselves, such calamitous failures could have been avoided. Instead, they chose denial over truth and paid a horrendous price.

Contrast that with Lego, a company confronted with a rapidly evolving marketplace and the threat of digital disruption. Lego's leadership could easily have clung to tradition, resisting change in loyalty to the past. Instead, they boldly questioned their internal assumptions, innovating courageously while sticking to their heritage. The result? Lego survived and thrived, demonstrating the incredible power of confronting and overcoming internal resistance.

Choosing the Path Forward

We all face small choices every day that reveal whether our inner enemies have mastered us or whether we have mastered them. In workplace meetings, will we defensively protect our egos or receptively hear criticism? When presented with opportunities for cooperation, will pride get in the way, or will humility allow for forward movement? Similarly, will we choose integrity or convenience when tempted to rationalize unethical shortcuts? In our relationships, will we hold on to prideful grudges or humble ourselves to forgive and rebuild?

As this book has shown, our capacity to win these internal struggles decides our potential, success, and, ultimately, our legacy. The best leaders, revered entrepreneurs, and fulfilled individuals are not those who repress their internal conflicts but those who courageously confront and overcome them.

Imagine your life five, ten, or even twenty years from now. How would you like to be remembered? As someone who succumbed to ego, pride, or perfectionism—or who fought these inner enemies valiantly, transforming them into tools for meaningful contribution? The biographies we have studied prove powerfully that the greatest hindrance to actualizing our highest potential is within. Overcoming these inner enemies—transforming ego into confidence, passion into vision, pride into humility, and loyalty into integrity—is the pathway to most tremendous success and genuine fulfillment.

Your Greatest Victory Awaits

The journey we've traveled together on these pages is a universal human journey. We all must confront our inner selves, enemies that battle us daily. But here's the great thing: within us is the power to overcome them. To know and master these inner enemies transforms them from agents of destruction into powerful allies.

Your most challenging battle is not with situations, rivals, or competitors but with your inner enemies—your own invisible enemies. You release incredible potential by fighting them honestly, courageously, and continuously. You become free to succeed and inspire, lead, and have a lasting effect on yourself, your organizations, and the world around you.

The decision is yours now. Will you boldly battle the enemy within? Will you direct your passion, control your ego, humble your pride, question your traditions, discipline your rationalizations, balance your loyalty, and embrace progress rather than perfection?

Your most significant victory is within your heart and mind, not on distant battlefields. The double-edged sword of your inner self is yours to wield wisely. Use it to defeat your inner enemies and leave your mark on history. It begins with one courageous step—walking to the mirror, seeing the enemy within, and choosing, from this day forward, who you are going to be.

Your struggle is already lost or won in the silent moments of introspection.

Choose wisely. Choose bravely. Choose intentionally.

Your narrative is waiting to be penned.

What will your legacy be?

APPENDIX

Educational Implications

Introduction

The Enemy delves into various psychological and sociological characteristics people display when facing extreme situations. Traits like resilience, adaptability, fear-driven choices, and social connections play a significant role in the classroom setting. Educators can create more effective teaching strategies by grasping how these traits influence learning, motivation, and group interactions. This chapter looks at how these traits can be applied in education, backed by empirical research and psychological insights to support its main points.

Resilience and Academic Success

One of the primary traits observed in The Enemy is resilience: the ability to withstand adversity and recover from setbacks. In educational psychology, research has shown that students who exhibit resilience tend to perform better in school despite facing economic, social, or personal challenges (Martin & Marsh, 2006). Studies suggest that resilience can be fostered through supportive teacher-student relationships, structured learning environments, and growth mindset interventions (Dweck, 2006). Educators can help students navigate academic and personal hardships more effectively by integrating resilience-building strategies into curricula.

Adaptability and Learning Environments

One of the standout traits from The Enemy is adaptability—something that today's students need more than ever. School isn't just about memorizing facts anymore; it requires students to constantly adjust to new challenges, from shifting curriculums to online learning environments. A study by Martin et al. (Martin et al., 2013) found that adaptable students tended to be more engaged and achieved higher overall.

When schools embrace strategies like problem-based learning, they can help students build that adaptability up. As Kolb (Kolb, 1984) suggested, experiential learning isn't just effective; it actively enhances student resilience and self-efficacy.

Fear and Decision-Making in Learning

Fear, primarily when it drives our decisions, greatly impacts how we learn and what motivates us. In The Enemy, for instance, the case studies often make choices based on immediate dangers, which is something we see in students who struggle with test anxiety or the fear of failing (Zeidner, 2007). Research in neurobiology shows that fear can mess with our thinking and working memory, leading to worse performance in school (Beilock & Ramirez, 2011).

But not all fear is bad. When kept at a manageable level, fear can motivate and push us toward our goals (Pekrun, Goetz, Titz, & Perry, 2002). That's where teachers come in. By working to create a classroom environment that is consistently low-pressure and high-support, we can help students manage their stress and, subsequently, their fear in healthier ways.

Social Bonding and Collaborative Learning

The Enemy highlights the role of social bonds and peer relationships in survival and success. In educational settings, social bonds are equally important. Students don't just learn from books; they learn from one another. Research shows that peer relationships can actually help our students boost motivation, deepen their understanding, and help them persist with challenges (Slavin, 1995).

Cooperative learning strategies like group projects, peer feedback, and collaborative assignments aren't just social activities; they've been shown to help students. These cooperative learning techniques improve retention and comprehension (Jonhson, Johnson & Smith, 2007). When students feel more connected to their friends, they're more likely to take risks and share ideas, but, most importantly, they're more likely to remain engaged in class.

Leadership and Classroom Dynamics

Leadership is another central theme in The Enemy and is just as important in the classroom. Giving students chances to lead, be it in the form of student governing, group presentations, or even classroom debates, allows us to foster autonomy, responsibility, and engagement (Kirkpatrick & Locke, 1991).

Leadership opportunities prepare students for future careers, and they improve communication and collaboration skills (Bass & Bass, 2008), which allows students to develop more confidence and capability in the present day, too.

Impulsivity and Risk-Taking in Learning

Teenagers are wired to take risks; it is an inevitable part of how their brains work (Steinberg, 2008). In The Enemy, many case studies look at acting impulsively and how this can lead to serious consequences. In real life, impulsivity can hurt academic performance, but that doesn't necessarily mean it is always bad.

When teachers give students the space to explore and experiment and even fail in low-stakes ways, it helps them to grow. Zhao (2012) argues that these opportunities improve students' critical thinking and can help spark innovation. The key is balance: providing structure and support while allowing room for curiosity and calculated risk.

Ethical Decision-Making and Moral Education

The moral dilemmas in The Enemy offer excellent material for helping students debate about right and wrong. According to Kohleberg's stages of moral development (1981), wrestling with complex ethical questions is a key part of growing up. When schools include discussions about ethics in subjects like literature, history, or social studies, students can build empathy and sharpen decision-making skills. Tools like role-playing, debates, and case studies like those used in The Enemy help make these lessons memorable. As Nucci& Narvaez (2008) suggest, students who engage with ethical questions early on are more likely to become thoughtful, responsible adults.

Conclusion

The traits explored in The Enemy—adaptability, courage, leadership, fear, and ethical decision making are deeply connected to what it means to grow and learn today. If we want to prepare students for tests and life, we need to create specialized learning environments that build resilience, encourage curiosity, and support personal development. That means helping them manage their fear instead of ignoring it, giving them a voice, letting them lead, and encouraging them to take low-stakes risks to learn from them.

Most importantly, it means remembering that students are whole people, not just grades and scores. When schools recognize this and nurture traits like empathy, adaptability, moral fortitude, and integrity, they create better students and noble citizens.

References

- Bass, B. M., & Bass, R. (2008). The Bass Handbook of Leadership: Theory, Research, and Managerial Applications. Free Press.
- Beilock, S. L., & Ramirez, G. (2011). On the interrelation of emotion and cognitive control: Implications for enhancing academic achievement. Psychology of Learning and Motivation, 55, 137-169.
- Dweck, C. S. (2006). Mindset: The New Psychology of Success. Random House.
- Johnson, D. W., Johnson, R. T., & Smith, K. A. (2007). The state of cooperative learning in postsecondary and professional settings. Educational Psychology Review, 19(1), 15-29.
- Kirkpatrick, S. A., & Locke, E. A. (1991). Leadership: Do traits matter? Academy of Management Perspectives, 5(2), 48-60.
- Kohlberg, L. (1981). The Philosophy of Moral Development. Harper & Row.
- Kolb, D. A. (1984). Experiential Learning: Experience as the Source of Learning and Development. Prentice Hall.
- Martin, A. J., & Marsh, H. W. (2006). Academic resilience and its psychological and educational correlates: A construct validity approach. Psychology in the Schools, 43(3), 267-281.
- Martin, A. J., Nejad, H. G., Colmar, S., & Liem, G. A. D. (2013). Adaptability: How students' responses to uncertainty and novelty predict their academic and non-academic outcomes. Journal of Educational Psychology, 105(3), 728-746.
- Masten, A. S. (2001). Ordinary magic: Resilience processes in development. American Psychologist, 56(3), 227-238.
- Nucci, L., & Narvaez, D. (2008). Handbook of Moral and Character Education. Routledge.
- Pekrun, R., Goetz, T., Titz, W., & Perry, R. P. (2002). Academic emotions in students' self-regulated learning and achievement: A program of qualitative and quantitative research. Educational Psychologist, 37(2), 91-105.
- Slavin, R. E. (1995). Cooperative Learning: Theory, Research, and Practice. Allyn & Bacon.
- Steinberg, L. (2008). A social neuroscience perspective on adolescent risk-taking. Developmental Review, 28(1), 78-106.
- Zeidner, M. (2007). Test anxiety in educational contexts: Concepts, findings, and future directions. In P. A. Schutz & R. Pekrun (Eds.), Emotion in Education (pp. 165-184). Academic Press.
- Zhao, Y. (2012). World Class Learners: Educating Creative and Entrepreneurial Students. Corwin Press.

Socio-Political Implications

Introduction

The Enemy explores resilience, adaptability, fear-driven decision-making, social bonding, leadership, impulsivity, and ethical reasoning and how people interact with each trait. These aren't just individual personal qualities and traits—they can shape how communities and political systems respond when things fall apart.

Understanding how these deeply personal traits translate into broader political structures, governance, collective action, and societies is essential for comprehending how communities and nations respond to crises, power dynamics, and social change.

Resilience and Political Stability

Our ability to bounce back after hardship is not just something people need as individuals—whole societies need it, too. Countries that can weather economic crashes, natural disasters, and political upheavals will experience less violent conflict and more effective governance (Norris, Stevens, Pfefferbaum, Wyche & Pfefferbaum, 2008).

Research suggests that countries with strong civil institutions—fair courts, free press, and reliable public services—foster resilience by protecting them from authoritarian tendencies (Diamond, 2008). On the other hand, societies that lack this resilience may succumb to political instability, especially under pressure (Acemoglu & Robinson, 2012).

Adaptability and Policy Innovation

In a fast-changing world, governments need to be able to adapt, just as individuals do. The Enemy highlights adaptability as a survival skill, and it is no different in politics. When policies and politicians fail to evolve with the times, systems stall and fail (Pierson, 2004).

Alternatively, in countries where flexibility is built into their governing models, like Scandinavia, there are significantly higher levels of social trust and, subsequently, more effective policymaking (Rothstein & Stolle, 2008). Political systems that allow for participatory governance allow quicker adaptation, as evidenced by instances like the swift pandemic response in countries like Taiwan and South Korea (Hale, Angrist, Goldszmidt, et al., 2012).

Fear-Driven Decision-Making and Authoritarianism

Fear is incredibly powerful, and when it spreads across society, it can change the political landscape entirely. History has shown that leaders often use fear to justify more control, fewer rights, and sweeping policies that would otherwise be outrageous (Altemeyer, 2006). After 9/11, for example, heightened fear led to the Patriot Act, which expanded government surveillance powers (Gould & Kor, 2010). Similarly, in economic crises, populist leaders have notoriously capitalized on fear to consolidate power, as we saw with the rise of nationalist movements in Europe (Mudde, 2019). Understanding how fear works on a psychological level can help us recognize when it is being used to manipulate us and push harmful agendas.

Social Bonding and Collective Action

The emphasis on social bonding in The Enemy highlights the power of collective action in political movements. Strong social connections are key to organizing and creating movements that push for justice (Putnam, 2000).

But while tight-knit communities can be a force for good, they can also create echo chambers and feed divisive ideologies; in fact, research shows that social movements with too rigid ideological boundaries can contribute to societal fragmentation (McAdam, Tarrow, Tilly, 2001). This is why it is essential to build solidarity while still ensuring that there is space for diverse viewpoints and voices within the community.

Leadership and Governance Effectiveness

Leadership in a crisis can make or break a country's response. This is seen within The Enemy, where leaders emerge through action. Political scientists talk about different leadership types, and every leadership style significantly impacts governance effectiveness. Transformational leaders inspire and innovate, while transactional leaders maintain stability with rule enforcement (Burns, 1978). The most effective leaders, according to research, do both. For example, Jacinda Ardern of New Zealand employed empathetic and transparent communication strategies during the COVID-19 pandemic, bolstering public trust (Wilson, 2020). Alternatively, authoritarian leaders who dismissed scientific expertise faced higher mortalities and unrest. Leadership matters—a lot. Understanding how leading works and impacts those around us is essential to maintain stable leadership.

Impulsivity and Political Decision-Making

Impulsivity is a recurring trait in The Enemy, and it has notable socio-political implications, especially in the decision-making process. Political leaders who make impulsive decisions without careful thought, particularly in foreign policy or crisis response, can often unintentionally create instability. Research has shown that cognitive biases—for example, overconfidence and present bias—influence political leaders' choices and distort their judgment (Kahneman & Tversky, 1979).

Take, for example, the Iraq War. The invasion in 2003 was later criticized for lacking foresight and contributing to long-term instability (Striglitz & Blimes, 2008). It is, therefore, crucial that in socio-political spheres, we avoid impulsivity and make decisions based on evidence-based approaches.

Ethical Reasoning and Political Integrity

The ethical choices in The Enemy reflect real-world challenges that leaders always face. Research in moral psychology suggests that ethical decision-making in politics is influenced by personal values and external pressures (Haidt, 2012). Research in moral psychology shows that ethics in politics aren't just about personal values but are also shaped by the systems in which people operate. When governments lack proper checks and balances, it's easier for corruption to take root, and once that happens, public trust can quickly disappear (Transparency International, 2021).

On the flip side, case studies highlight that nations with robust ethical frameworks, such as Sweden and Denmark, maintain higher levels of transparency and subsequent stability (Holmberg & Rothstein, 2011), proving that by integrating ethical reasoning into political education and leadership training, we can enhance accountability and democratic resilience.

Conclusion

Each of the traits previously examined in The Enemy—resilience, adaptability, fear-driven decision-making, social bonding, leadership, impulsivity, and ethical reasoning—carries important and undeniable socio-political implications. They are more than just survival tools. They're the key to understanding how societies function, especially in times of upheaval. When we apply the lessons from The Enemy to real-world politics, we can see just how much individual behavior shapes collective outcomes. By promoting strong leadership, flexibility, ethical standards, and community bonds; we can build systems that don't just survive crises but that come out stronger.

References

- Acemoglu, D., & Robinson, J. A. (2012). Why Nations Fail: The Origins of Power, Prosperity, and Poverty. Crown.
- Altemeyer, B. (2006). The Authoritarians. Lulu Press.
- Burns, J. M. (1978). Leadership. Harper & Row.
- Diamond, L. (2008). The Spirit of Democracy: The Struggle to Build Free Societies Throughout the World. Henry Holt.
- Feldman, S. (2003). Enforcing social conformity: A theory of authoritarianism. Political Psychology, 24(1), 41-74.
- Gould, E. D., & Klor, E. F. (2010). Does terrorism work? Quarterly Journal of Economics, 125(4), 1459-1510.
- Hale, T., Angrist, N., Goldszmidt, R., et al. (2021). A global panel database of pandemic policies (Oxford COVID-19 Government Response Tracker). Nature Human Behaviour, 5, 529-538.
- Haidt, J. (2012). The Righteous Mind: Why Good People Are Divided by Politics and Religion. Pantheon Books.
- Holmberg, S., & Rothstein, B. (2011). Good Government: The Relevance of Political Science. Edward Elgar Publishing.
- Howard, P. N., & Hussain, M. M. (2013). Democracy's Fourth Wave? Digital Media and the Arab Spring. Oxford University Press.
- Transparency International. (2021). Corruption Perceptions Index. Retrieved from www.transparency.org
- Wilson, N. (2020). Public health lessons from New Zealand's COVID-19 response. The Lancet Public Health, 5(11), e569-e570.

The TRAPPED Model: Breaking Through Internal Barriers to Unlock Potential

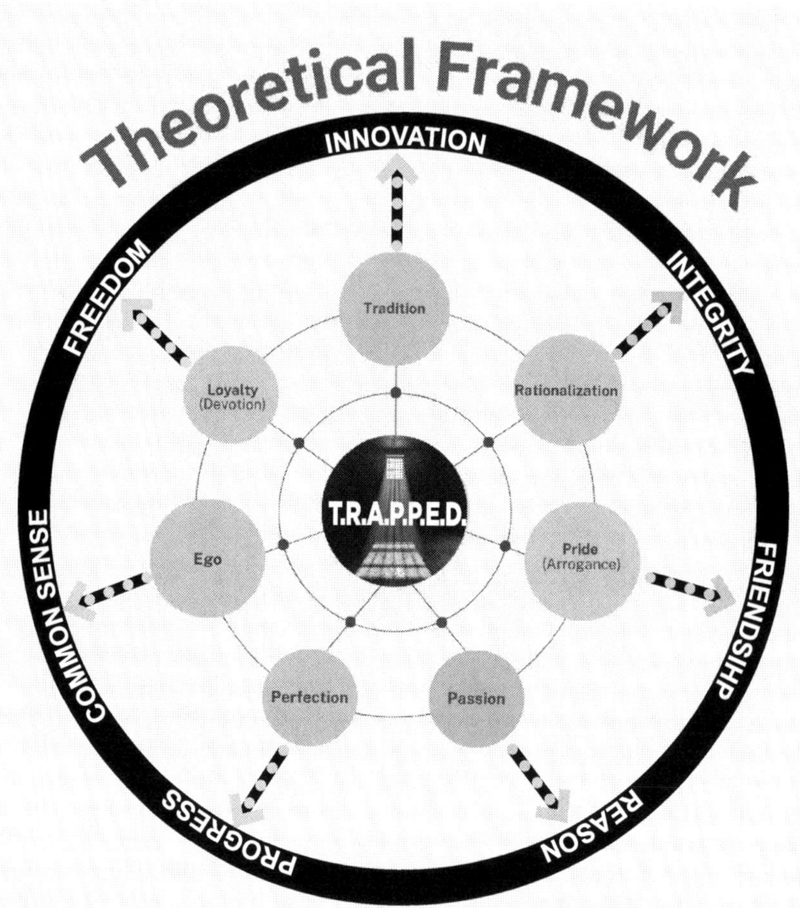

Understanding the TRAPPED Framework

Breaking Through Internal Barriers to Unlock Potential

A useful theoretical framework for understanding how our inherent characteristics, which we frequently view as our strengths, can actually be limiting us is the TRAPPED Model. It separates things into Tradition, Rationalization, Arrogance, Passion, Exactingness, and Devotion—all of which, while initially enticing, can backfire if left unchecked.

The fundamental idea of this model is that there is an extreme form that becomes a barrier for every admirable attribute. What begins as a guiding principle can become a strict restriction if not intentionally controlled.

Every component of TRAPPED stands for an internal "enemy" that challenges a crucial quality needed for development and success. Each component is covered in detail below, along with their connections and how they affect leadership, decision-making, and personal growth.

T – Tradition (Enemy of Innovation)

The Trap

Tradition offers cultural identity, continuity, and stability. However, clinging too firmly to the past can impede progress. Any kind of creativity and adaptability may be discouraged due to this defiant resistance to change. Tradition-bound individuals and institutions frequently hold fast to outdated practices out of a fear of the unknown that comes with novel concepts.

How It Relates to Innovation

- Tradition thrives on the past; innovation thrives on the future.
- Traditional thinking resists disruption; innovation requires breaking norms.

- Tradition seeks comfort in precedent; innovation embraces Xthe unknown.

Breaking Free

It is necessary to question presumptions and foster an attitude of constant improvement to escape the trap of tradition. This entails challenging established customs, trying out novel approaches, and accepting discomfort as a sign of development.

R – Rationalization (Enemy of Integrity)

The Trap

Everyone occasionally engages in rationalization, the inner voice that tries to justify a poor decision, frequently to stay comfortable or escape accountability. However, when this becomes a habit, it undermines organizational and personal integrity by providing a fictitious excuse for unethical behavior or poor performance.

How It Relates to Integrity

- Integrity requires accountability; rationalization deflects blame.
- Integrity thrives on truth; rationalization distorts reality.
- Integrity demands consistency; rationalization allows convenient exceptions.

Breaking Free

Radical honesty is necessary to escape rationalization. This entails facing hard realities, owning up to errors, and, even in the face of difficulty, coordinating actions with fundamental principles.

A – Arrogance (Ego & Pride Combined) – Enemy of Common Sense & Friendship

The Trap

Typically, arrogance stems from an exaggerated self-perception that can impair our judgment. Overconfidence can result in poor decisions, a refusal to hear other people out, and an unwarranted sense of pride. When left unchecked, this pride keeps people from acknowledging the contributions of others or owning up to their mistakes.

How It Relates to Common Sense & Friendship

- Common sense requires open-mindedness; arrogance assumes it knows best.
- Friendship requires humility and reciprocity; arrogance creates isolation.
- Common sense encourages adaptability; arrogance clings to self-righteousness.

Breaking Free

The antidote to arrogance is humility and self-awareness. Seek feedback, listen to diverse perspectives, and recognize that wisdom often comes from acknowledging what you don't know.

P – Passion (Enemy of Reason)

The Trap

The most common cause of arrogance is an exaggerated self-perception that impairs judgment. Excessive self-esteem can result in poor decisions, a refusal to hear other people out, and an unwarranted sense of pride. Unchecked pride keeps people from acknowledging the contributions of others or owning up to their mistakes.

How It Relates to Reason

- Reason provides balance; unchecked passion leads to recklessness.
- Passion can cloud judgment; reason ensures clarity.
- Passion drives energy; reason provides direction.

Breaking Free

Balance passion with strategic planning and critical thinking to ensure it enhances rather than detracts. Rather than replacing reason, passion should serve as a motivating tool.

E – Exactingness (Perfection) – Enemy of Progress

The Trap

Perfectionism frequently poses as a positive quality, but it usually just paralyzes people. The desire for perfection breeds an innate fear of failing, which results in missed opportunities and procrastination.

How It Relates to Progress

- Progress thrives on iteration; perfectionism demands an unattainable ideal.
- Perfectionism delays action; progress values momentum.
- Progress learns from mistakes; perfectionism fears them.

Breaking Free

To overcome perfectionism, one must change their perspective from one of perfection to one of advancement. Instead of waiting for the ideal circumstances, concentrate on iteration, learning, and action.

D – Devotion (Loyalty) – Enemy of Freedom The Trap

Although loyalty is a positive quality, excessive loyalty can result in blind allegiance. Over-dedication to individuals, ideologies, or groups—even when they are no longer in one's best interests – restricts one's freedom and ability to develop personally.

How It Relates to Freedom

- Freedom allows choice; excessive loyalty binds individuals to obligations.
- Freedom fosters independent thinking; blind devotion suppresses dissent.

- Freedom encourages growth; excessive loyalty keeps individuals stuck.

Breaking Free

True loyalty should be deliberate and voluntary instead of being a restriction. Evaluate whether your commitments align with your values and allow yourself to let go when needed.

The Compounding Effect of TRAPPED

These internal barriers are rarely isolated. They reinforce each other, creating a cycle of stagnation:

- A leader trapped in tradition (T) may rationalize (R) their resistance to change.
- An arrogant (A) individual may refuse to acknowledge how their passion (P) is leading them astray.
- A perfectionist (E) may stay loyal (D) to an unrealistic standard, never taking action.

The deeper one is trapped, the harder it is to break free. Recognizing this cycle is the first step toward change.

Breaking Free: The Journey to Your Best Self

The TRAPPED Model is not about self-condemnation—it's about self-awareness. Recognizing these internal traps leads to personal and professional transformation.

Steps to Break Free

1. Identify Your Greatest Trap – Which trait limits you the most?
2. Acknowledge Its Impact – How does it hold you back?
3. Apply the Opposite Trait – Cultivate the trait it suppresses.
4. Commit to Small Changes – Consistent effort leads to long-term growth.

Breaking free from TRAPPED means unlocking the ability to think freely, act with integrity, collaborate effectively, make balanced decisions, embrace progress, and live without constraints.

Release Yourself from Capture and Realize Your Complete Potential.

Made in the USA
Columbia, SC
10 June 2025